JUDAISM, MEDICINE, AND HEALING

JUDAISM, MEDICINE, AND HEALING

RONALD H. ISAACS

JASON ARONSON INC.
NORTHVALE, NEW JERSEY
JERUSALEM

This book was set in 12 pt. Corona by Alabama Book Composition of Deatsville, Alabama and printed and bound by Book-mart Press, Inc. of North Bergen, NJ.

Library of Congress Cataloging-in-Publication Data

Isaacs, Ronald H.
    Judaism, medicine, and healing / by Ronald H. Isaacs.
        p.   cm.
    Includes bibliographical references and index.
    ISBN 0-7657-9997-9 (alk. paper)
    1. Health—Religious aspects—Judaism. 2. Medicine—Religious aspects—Judaism. 3. Medical laws and legislation (Jewish law).
    4. Body, Human, in rabbinical literature. 5. Jews—Medicine.
    I. Title.
    BM538.H43I83   1998
    296.3′76—dc21   97–31784

Printed in the United States of America. Jason Aronson Inc. offers books and cassettes. For information and catalog write to Jason Aronson Inc., 230 Livingston Street, Northvale, NJ 07647-1726, or visit our website: http://www.aronson.com

For Dr. Mark Gold

In appreciation of your generosity
and many kindnesses

Contents

Introduction

Health and healing are universal human concerns. Many traditions proffer advice on medical matters from their various perspectives. Jews have a particularly rich treasury of resources in medicine and its ethics that provide both general principles and specific instructions in certain areas.

In Judaism, God owns everything—including our bodies, which are on loan to humans during their lives and returned to God at the time of death. This underlying principle of ownership of our bodies produces not only prohibitions, but obligations that are related to the maintenance of good health and healing. These include taking care of our bodies, good hygiene, sleep, exercise, and diet. Deuteronomy 4:15 sums up the attitude of Judaism toward the care of one's body: "Take good heed of your souls."

In recent years, the art of healing has taken on a new dimension in Judaism with the creation of The

National Center for Jewish Healing. This organization offers healing prayer services and spiritual support groups for those who are ill and in need of healing. Today it serves as a catalyst for more than fifteen Jewish healing centers now evolving around the United States and Canada.

This volume will explore and examine classical and contemporary Judaic sources and issues, from biblical times to the present, related to health, medicine, and healing. Topics include the laws of *bikkur cholim* (visiting the sick); sources related to the obligation to heal in Judaism; images of God as Healer; the ten healing psalms of Rabbi Nachman of Breslov; other healing psalms; healing texts and the liturgy; Jewish views of exercise, diet, cleanliness, hygiene, and care of one's body; Jewish views of the physician; Maimonides' oath and his prayer for physicians; and healing in Jewish legend and other rabbinic texts.

BIKKUR CHOLIM: VISITING THE SICK

These are the deeds that yield fruit and continue to yield fruit in time to come . . . visiting
the sick (*Shabbat* 127a).

The following ancient Jewish legend teaches an
important lesson related to the power of people
serving other people.

A righteous man was permitted by God to attain
foreknowledge of the world-to-come. In a celestial
palace he was ushered into a large room, where he
beheld people seated at a banquet table. The table
was laden with the most delectable foods, but not a
morsel had been touched. The righteous man gazed
in wonder at the people seated at the table. They
were emaciated with hunger and moaned constantly
for food, even though the delicious viands were
before them.

"If they are hungry, why is it that they do not
partake of the food that is before them?" asked the
righteous one of his heavenly guide. "They cannot
feed themselves," said the guide. "If you will no-
tice, each one has his arms strapped straight, so
that no matter how he tries, he cannot get the food

3

into his mouth." "Truly, this is hell," said the righteous one as they left the hall.

The heavenly attendant escorted him across the hall into another room, and the righteous one observed another table equally as beautiful, and also laden with delicacies. Here he noticed that those seated around the table were well-fed, contented, and joyous. To his amazement, he discerned that these people, too, had their arms strapped straight. Turning to his guide, he asked in perplexity: "How is it, then, that they are so well fed, since they are unable to transport the food to their mouths?" "Behold," said the heavenly guide. The righteous one looked closely, and beheld that each one was feeding the other. "In truth," he exclaimed, "this is truly heaven." "In truth it is," agreed the attendant. "As you can see, the difference between heaven and hell is a matter of cooperation and serving one's fellow human being."

For Jews, *bikkur cholim* (visiting the sick) is one important way of serving one's fellow human being. Visiting the sick is much more than simply a social act that is to be commended. Rather, it has the status of a *mitzvah*, a religious obligation, and it is counted in the Talmud among the religious duties for which no limit has been prescribed (*Shabbat* 127a). God Himself is said to have visited Abraham during his illness. The rabbis of the Talmud found reference to this visit in Genesis 18:1, where we are told that God appeared to Abraham soon after his circumcision.

The Bible commands, "And you shall walk in God's ways" (Deuteronomy 28:9). A person is expected to pattern himself upon God's ways. Thus, just as God visited Abraham immediately following his circumcision, so too the Jew has the obligation to visit the sick.

Visiting the sick is, according to the Talmud, one of the precepts for the fulfillment of which a person is rewarded in both this world and the world-to-come. Ben Sira (7:35) counsels: "Do not hesitate to visit a person who is sick."

Visiting the sick is considered to be one of the supreme acts of holiness, because one's visit brings both physical and psychological relief and healing to the sick person. According to a talmudic statement (*Nedarim* 40a), whoever visits a sick person helps that person to recover. A visit to a sick person can help calm and lift the patient's spirit, engendering a feeling of care, warmth, and love.

The Talmud tells how Rabbi Akiva once visited a student who had become ill. No one else bothered to visit the disciple, and, as a result, his house was most untidy. Rabbi Akiva did all that was needed, even sweeping the man's floors. When the disciple recovered, he attributed his restored health to Akiva's visit. By preparing his home for a return to life's daily routine, he said, Akiva had strengthened his will to get well.

Jewish tradition also teaches that it is important to allow others to help us when we are sick. For example, the Talmud (*Nedarim* 39b–40a) tells the story of Rabbi Yochanan, who once visited Rabbi Chanina when he was ill. When Chanina complained about his suffering, Rabbi Yochanan suggested that he repeat to himself the same encouraging words he had spoken to such good effect when Rabbi Yochanan was ill. Chanina replied: "When I was free of suffering, I helped others. But now that I suffer, I must ask others to help me." This story is a reminder that one should know when to give and when and how to receive, and that, in receiving, one is also often giving.

During the Middle Ages, much kindness was shown by those visiting the ill. It was quite common, after the synagogue service on the Sabbath morning, for worshippers to pay regular visits to the sick before they returned home to partake of their meal. There was also a customary etiquette to visiting the sick. Short visits—rather than lengthy ones— were encouraged, and visitors were instructed not to visit when the sick person was in extreme pain.

In modern times, the religious duty to visit the sick has become an obligation for professionals. When a person becomes ill, he or she is treated by a network of health-care facilities and medical professionals. In addition, the patient is generally visited by a clergyperson of that patient's faith, who brings comfort to patients in local hospitals and nursing facilities. Such conditions are of recent origin. For centuries, the Jewish people sought to give emotional support to those who were ill as well as to provide medical care to the extent that it was available. There were *bikkur cholim* societies whose function it was to visit those confined by illness. Today, many synagogues and Jewish communities have their own *bikkur cholim* groups, which afford members of their congregations who are ill, both comfort and friendship.

The *mitzvah* of *bikkur cholim* is necessarily much different from the typical social visit. The famous philosopher and commentator Nachmanides explains that the obligation consists of two parts: (1) an endeavor to determine whether the patient requires care, and the actual provision of such medical and nursing care as is necessary; and (2) prayer on behalf of the patient. Nachmanides goes on to say that one who visits the sick and does not pray on his behalf has not fulfilled the *mitzvah*.

It is customary, upon visiting the sick, to extend the prayerful wish that the patient be granted a complete recovery from his or her illness. The words for a complete healing are *Refuah shlayma*. This phrase is taken from the eighth benediction of the daily Amidah, in which the worshiper petitions God to heal all who are ill.

WHY VISIT THE SICK?

Visiting the sick often cheers patients and inspires them with comfort and with hope. Here are a couple of rabbinic selections that illuminate the ancient rabbinic thinking vis-à-vis the reason for visiting those that are ill.

Visiting the Sick Alleviates Pain

Rabbi Acha son of Chanina said: "One who visits the sick takes away one-sixtieth of that person's pain." They said to him: "If so, let sixty people visit him and restore him to health." He replied: "The principle of decreasing illness by one-sixtieth is the same as the principle of distribution of property among female heirs: as the tenth spoken of in the school of Rabbi. . . ." For it was taught: "Rabbi said, 'A daughter who enjoys maintenance from her brothers' estate receives a tenth of the estate.'" They said to Rabbi: "If so, if a man leaves ten daughters and one son, the son receives nothing." He replied: "The first to marry receives a tenth of the estate, the second a tenth of the remaining, the third a tenth of what remains" (*Nedarim* 39b).

Visiting the Sick Gives Life

When Rav Dimi came, he said: "He who visits the sick causes him to live, while he who does not causes him to die." How does he cause this? Shall we say that he who visits the sick prays that he may live, while he who does not prays that he should die? "That he should die." Can you really think that someone would pray so? But say thus: "He who does not visit the sick prays neither that he may live nor that he may die" (*Nedarim* 40a).

In the first passage we learn of the belief that each person who visits a sick person takes away one-sixtieth of that person's illness. Regarding the power of healing inherent in visiting the sick, it is quite likely that Rabbi Acha believed that when a sick person believes that people care about his or her welfare, that person feels better.

The second passage likely relates to a talmudic statement made by Rabbi Akiva that "one who does not visit the sick is like a shedder of blood"

(*Nedarim* 40a). Rav Dimi appears to be making the point that when one does not visit the sick, one is not showing concern for that person's welfare. The passage also clearly alludes to the purpose of visiting the sick, which includes cheering patients, rendering them any service, inspiring them with hope, and praying for their welfare.

WHEN AND HOW LONG TO VISIT

The Best Times to Visit the Sick

Visitors must be sensitive to the patient's needs and condition. The following passage and the passage in the next section relate to the timing of visiting the sick and the amount of time that a visitor ought to stay with a patient.

Rav Shisha son of Rav Idi said: "One should not visit the sick during the first three or the last three hours of the day, lest he thereby omit to pray for him." During the first three hours of the day, the sick person's illness is alleviated; in the last three hours, his sickness is strongest (*Nedarim* 40a). [The modern physician is well aware of the accuracy of this statement. Fever is usually lower in the morning and higher in the evening in a patient with a febrile illness.]

This passage may imply that if the visitor sees the sick person during the first three hours, he may think that the sick person is nearly well and not in need of visitors. If, on the other hand, he visits during the last three hours, he may think that the patient is about to die. In either case, the temporary change in the sick person's condition may cause the visitor to treat him in ways that are inappropriate to his condition.

Limit Your Stay

The next selection is a statement by Rabbi Eliezer, an eleventh-century scholar and teacher:

> Be zealous in visiting the sick, for sympathy lightens pain. . . . Pray for him, and leave. Do not fatigue him by staying too long, for his malady is heavy enough already. Enter cheerfully, for his heart and eyes are on those who come in.

Rabbi Eliezer is providing sound psychological advice, for visitors often do overextend their stays, causing fatigue to the sick person, which may be injurious to the health.

WHO SHOULD VISIT WHOM?

Should people visit ill people that they don't know? Is it enough to visit our sick friends and relatives? The following passages shed light upon these questions and other matters related to the question of who should visit whom.

The Great Should Visit the Humble

Judah Ha-Chasid, a twelfth-century moralist, said: "Even the great should visit the humble. If a poor man and a rich man fall ill at the same time, and many go to the rich man to pay him honor, then go to the poor man, even if the rich man is a scholar" (*Sefer Chasidim*).

Relatives and Close Friends Should Visit First

Relatives and close friends visit as soon as a person becomes sick; others should visit after the first three days of illness (Jerusalem Talmud, *Pe'ah* 3:7). Here we see the preference for visitors who are closely acquainted with the invalid during the early days of the illness. The reasons for this are that during the first three days a patient may not be feeling very well, and that those most closely acquainted with him will be the ones most likely to know how best to tend to his needs.

Whom to Visit and Whom Not to Visit

This statement is taken from the talmudic tractate *Nedarim* 41a.

Samuel said: "Only a sick person who is feverish may be visited." What does this exclude? It excludes those whom it has been taught by Rabbi Yose ben Parta in Rabbi Eliezer's name: "One must not visit those suffering with bowel trouble, or with eye disease or from headaches." Now, the first is logical, the reason being through embarrassment. But what is the reason of the other two? On account of Rabbi Judah's dictum: "Speech is injurious to the eyes and to people suffering from headaches."

WHAT TO DO DURING THE VISIT

The following rabbinic advice relates to what a visitor ought to do during the visit itself. From these selections we learn that praying on behalf of the sick is an expectation. In addition, several of the texts imply that if one lovingly acquiesces in one's sufferings, one's reward in the world-to-come will be great. We also learn that touch may be quite important to the healing process, and that healing requires much faith and commitment. From the last selection we learn that bringing things (refreshments and the like) can help awaken the souls of those who are ill.

What to Say When Visiting the Sick

When Rabbi Judah visited the sick, he said, "May the Almighty have compassion upon you and the sick of Israel." Rabbi Yose said, "May the Almighty have compassion upon you in the midst of Israel." Sometimes Rabbi Elazar would say, "The Almighty visit you in peace." At other times, he said, "The Almighty remember you in peace" (*Shabbat* 12b).

Visiting the Sick Uplifts Them

Rabbi Chiyya ben Abba fell ill, and Rabbi Yochanan went to visit him. He said to him: "Are your sufferings welcome to you?" He replied: "Neither they nor their reward." He said to him: "Give me your hand." He gave him his hand and he raised him. Why was Rabbi Yochanan unable to raise himself? They replied: "The prisoner cannot free himself from jail."

Rabbi Yochanan once fell ill, and Rabbi Chanina went to visit him. He said to him: "Are your sufferings welcome to you?" He replied: "Neither they nor their reward." He said to him: "Give me your hand." He gave him his hand and he raised him. Why would not Rabbi Yochanan raise himself? They replied: "The prisoner cannot free himself from jail."

Rabbi Eleazar fell ill and Rabbi Yochanan went to visit him. He noticed that he was lying in a dark room, and he bared his arm and light radiated from it. Thereupon he noticed that Rabbi Eleazar was weeping, and he said to him: "Why do you weep? Is it because you did not study enough Torah? Surely we learned: The one who sacrifices much and the one who sacrifices little have the same merit, provided that the heart is directed to heaven. Is it perhaps lack of sustenance? Not everybody has the privilege to enjoy two tables [i.e., learning and wealth]. Is it perhaps because of the lack of children? This is the bone of my tenth son." He replied to him: "I am weeping on account of this beauty, that is going to rot in the earth." He said to him: "On that account you surely have reason to weep," and they both wept. In the meanwhile he said to him:

"Are your sufferings welcome to you?" He replied: "Neither they nor their reward." He said to him: "Give me your hand," and he gave him his hand and he raised him (*Berachot* 5b).

Never Visit the Sick Empty-Handed

"When you visit a sick person who is without means, do not go to him with empty hands. When he awakens, be quick to offer him refreshments and he will esteem it as though you did uphold and restore his soul" (Rabbi Eliezer of Worms).

SUMMARY OF LAWS RELATED TO VISITING THE SICK

The following is a summary of laws for visiting the sick. The source of these is the *Kitzur Shulchan Aruch: The Condensed Code of Jewish Law* compiled by Rabbi Solomon Ganzfried.

1. All Are Obligated to Visit the Sick: When a person gets sick, it is the duty of every person to visit him, for we find that the Blessed Holy One visits the sick. As our rabbis of blessed memory explained [*Baba Metzia* 86b] the verse (Genesis 18:1): "And God appeared unto him in the plains of Mamre," from this is inferred that God came to visit Abraham because he was sick. Relatives and friends who are accustomed to visit the person often should visit as soon as they hear of his sickness.

Strangers should not call immediately, but should wait three days, in order not to spoil his chances of recovery by attaching to him the designation cf a patient. If, however, one becomes suddenly ill, even strangers should visit him immediately. Even a great person should visit a less important one, even many times during the day. It is meritorious to visit a sick person as frequently as possible, providing that it does not weary the sick person. One should not visit a sick enemy, nor should one come to comfort him in his mourning, for he may think that he rejoices at his calamity. One may, however, attend his funeral, and he need not fear that people will think that he rejoices at his downfall, since this is the end of every mortal.

2. The Posture of the Visitor: When the patient lies upon the ground, the visitor must not sit upon a chair, which is more elevated, because the Divine Presence is above the head of the sick, as it is written [Psalms 41:4]: "God supports him upon the bed of illness." But when the invalid lies in bed, the visitor may sit on a chair or on a bench.

3. The Importance of Prayer: The essential reason for the precept of visiting the sick is to look to his needs, to see what is necessary to be done for him, and to pray for mercy on his behalf. If one visited a sick person and did not pray for him, he did not fulfill his duty.

4. What Language to Use and What to Say When Praying for the Ill: If one prays in the presence of the sick person, one may say the prayer in any language, because one is praying before the Divine Presence, Who is at the bedside of the sick. If, however, one prays in the absence of the sick person, and the prayer is brought up by ministering angels who do not regard all languages, one should pray in Hebrew and include him among the sick of Israel; for, by including him with all the others, the prayer will be more readily heard because of the collective merit of the multitude. In praying, one says: "May the Omnipresent have mercy upon him among all the sick of Israel"; on the Sabbath, one adds: "This is the Sabbath. We are forbidden to complain; healing is sure to come; God's mercy is great. God's seat is in peace."

5. What to Talk About When Visiting the Sick: Visitors must use judgment and tact when talking to the sick person, so as not to give him false hopes or cause him to despair. They should encourage him to talk about his affairs and to state whether he had loaned to others, or had deposited anything with others or others with him. The sick person should be given to understand that to impart such information will not hasten his death.

6. Never Mix Thoughts of Mourning When Visiting the Sick: The patient should not be informed of the death of a member of his family, because it may disconcert him. Even if he becomes aware of it, he should not be told to rend his garments, lest it aggravate his anxiety. One should neither weep nor mourn in the presence of a sick person, whether the dead be a member of his family or a stranger, lest he fear that he, too, will pass away. Those who comfort mourners in the presence of a sick person should be silenced.

7. Visiting Those Afflicted with Intestinal Problems Is Prohibited: We must not visit a person who is afflicted with intestinal pains, so as not to embarrass him, or one who is troubled with his eyes, or one who has a headache, or any person who is gravely ill, and to whom conversation is difficult. But we should call at an outer room, inquire regarding the patient's condition, and ascertain whether the patient is in need of anything. We should take an interest in the person's condition and pray for mercy on his behalf.

8. Instructions for One Who Has Two Precepts to Perform: One who has two precepts to perform— namely, visiting a sick person and comforting a mourner—and is able to attend both, should first visit the sick, so that one may pray for mercy on his behalf. If one is unable to fulfill both duties, one should fulfill that of comforting the mourner, as this is an act of loving-kindness toward both the living and the dead.

9. The Importance of Visiting a Non-Jew Who Is Ill: A non-Jew should be visited during his illness for the sake of preserving peaceful relations.

10. A Dying Person Must Confess: It is expounded in the Sifri (Numbers 5–6): "Rabbi Nathan said:

'From the verse [Numbers 5:6]: "And that soul be guilty, then shall they confess," a conclusion can be drawn, that all dying persons must confess.'"

11. Text of the Confessional: A brief form of confession is as follows: "I acknowledge unto You, O God and God of my ancestors, that both my cure and my death are in Your hand. May it be Your will to grant me a perfect healing. Yet, if You have decreed that I should die, may my death expiate all the sins, iniquities, and transgressions that I have committed perversely before You, and grant me a portion in *Gan Eden* and cause me to merit the life of the world-to-come, which is reserved for the righteous." If the invalid wishes to make a lengthy confession, like the one for Yom Kippur, he may do so.

OTHER NOTABLE TEXTS AND QUOTES ABOUT VISITING THE SICK

1. Imitating God: Rabbi Chama said in the name of Rabbi Chanina: What does it mean, "You shall walk after the Lord your God" [Deuteronomy 13:5]? Is it possible for a person to walk and follow God's presence? Does not the Torah also say: "For the Lord your God is a consuming fire" [Deuteronomy 4:24]? But it means to walk after the attributes of the Holy Blessed One. Just as God clothes the naked, so you must too, as it says, "And God made the man and his wife leather coverings and clothed them" [Genesis 3:21]. The Holy Blessed One visits the ill, as it says, "And God visited him [Abraham] in Elonei Mamre"; so too must you visit the ill (*Sotah* 14a). . . .

2. Thoughts on the Messiah: Rabbi Joshua ben Levi met Elijah sitting at the opening of the cave of Rabbi Shimon bar Yochai. . . . He said to Elijah, "When will the Messiah come?" He answered, "Go and ask Him Himself." "Where is he sitting?" "At the gates of the city." "What is his sign that I may recognize him?" "He sits among the poor who suffer from their wounds." All of them unbind and rebind their wounds in one act. But he unbinds and rebinds [each wound] separately, saying, "Should I be wanted, these all being dressed at once should not delay me."

3. When a Teacher Is Sick: When God revealed Himself, the Holy Blessed One stood and Abraham sat, as it says, ". . . And he was sitting in the doorway. . . ." It is the custom of the world that when a student is sick and the teacher goes to visit, other students go first and say, "There is a delegation of the teacher to the house of the patient," meaning that the teacher wishes to visit the student. Not so the Holy Blessed One. When Abraham was circumcised and was in pain from the circumcision, He told the messengers to go and visit. But before they arrived, God came in first, as the Torah says, "And God appeared to him," and after that,

"And he lifted his eyes and saw three. . . ." Is there no greater Humble One than this (Midrash Tanchuma Vayera 2)?

4. The Importance of Non-Verbal Communication: A person can visit the sick even if he does not speak a word, such as when the patient is sleeping. For it will probably be that when he is told that so-and-so came to see him, this will bring to him ease of the spirit (*Tzitz Eliezer* 8:5).

5. Visiting the Sick Has No Set Reward: It was taught: Visiting the sick has no set amount. What is meant by this statement? Rabbi Joseph thought it means that there is no set amount for its reward [i.e., its reward is unlimited]. Abaye said to him: "Does anyone have the set amount of the reward for the *mitzvot*? Do we not learn: Be careful with an easy *mitzvah* as with a heavy one, for you do not know the reward of the *mitzvot*." But Abaye said: "It must mean, 'Even the greater goes on to visit the smaller.'" Raba said: "No set amount means one can visit even a hundred times a day" (*Nedarim* 39b).

6. Visiting the Sick Can Save One from Hellish Punishment: Rav says: "One who visits the sick will be delivered from the punishments of *Gehenna*," for it is written, "Happy is he that considers the poor [*dal*, in Hebrew], the Lord will deliver him in the day of evil." "The poor" means none other than the sick, as it is written, "He will cut me off from pining sickness" [*mi-dalah*] [Isaiah 38:12] or from this verse, "Why are you so poorly [*dal*], you son of the King" [2 Samuel 13:4]? Evil refers to *Gehenna* for it is written, "The Lord has made all things for Himself, yea even the wicked, for the day of evil" [Proverbs 16:4]. Now, if one does visit, what is his reward? You ask, What is his reward? Even as has been said, "He will be delivered from the punishment of *Gehenna*." But what is his reward in this world? "God will preserve him and keep him alive, let him be called happy in the land. And You will not deliver him to the greed of his enemies." "God will preserve him," from the evil urge; "And keep him alive," saving him from his sufferings. "Let him be called happy in the land," that all will take pride in him; "And You will not deliver him into the greed of his enemies," that he may procure friends like Naaman's who healed his leprosy, and not chance upon friends like Rehaboam's, who divided his kingdom (*Nedarim* 40a).

7. God Sustains the Sick: Rabin said in the name of Rav: "From where do we know that the Holy Blessed One sustains the sick? As it says, God will support him upon his bed of illness" [Psalms 41]. Rabin also said in the name of Rav: "From where do we know that the Divine Presence rests above the invalid's bed? From the verse, "God will support him upon his bed of illness" (*Nedarim* 40a).

8. The Sick Versus the Dangerously Ill: What is the difference between one who is sick and one who is considered dangerously ill? One who is merely sick is so in the normal way. "Dangerously ill" refers to one whose sickness came suddenly. For a normal sickness, relatives visit immediately, and those more distant visit after three days. But if the sickness came suddenly, both relatives and those more distant can visit immediately. Rav Huna, Rabbi Pinchas, and Rabbi Chilkiah desisted from visiting Rabbi Yossi for three days. Rabbi Yossi said to them, "Through me must you fulfill this teaching" (Jerusalem Talmud *Gittin* 6:5; Jerusalem Talmud *Pe'ah*, Ch. 3).

9. Proper Posture When Visiting the Sick: It was taught: "One who enters to visit the sick should not sit on a bed or a bench or a chair, but should enrobe himself and sit on the ground, for the Divine Presence rests above the bed of the patient, as it says [Psalm 41], "God will support him upon his bed of illness" (*Nedarim* 40a).

10. The Importance to the Ill of Forgiveness of Sins: Rabbi Alexandri said in the name of Rabbi Chiyya ben Abba: A patient does not recover from sickness until all his sins are forgiven, as it is written, "Who forgives all your sins, Who heals all your diseases" [Psalms 103:3]. Rav Hamnuna said: He then returns to the days of his youth, for it is written, "His flesh shall be fresher than a child's, he shall return to the days of his youth" [Job 33:25] (*Nedarim* 41:4).

11. Asking for Mercy: Rabbi Pinchas ben Chama expounded: One who has an ill person in his home should go to a wise man so that he may ask mercy for him, as it says [Proverbs 16:14]: "The anger of a king is like messengers of death, but a wise man will pacify it" (*Baba Batra* 116a).

12. The Power of Personal Prayer: The prayer of a sick person for his own recovery avails more than the prayer of another (Genesis Rabbah 53:14).

13. Rich, Poor, and Torah Scholars: If both a rich man and a pauper are sick, the rich man will have many visitors who want to pay their respects. Therefore, one should visit the poor man. And even if the rich man is also a Torah scholar, one should still visit the poor man, because the rich scholar will have a room full of visitors, whereas the poor man will have none. But if both the Torah scholar and the poor man are needy, then the honor of the Torah scholar takes precedence. If he is a Torah scholar who is not God-fearing, whereas the poor man is God-fearing, the God-fearing one has priority, because it says, "The beginning of wisdom is the fear of God" [Psalms 11:10] (*Sefer Chasidim*).

14. Be Careful When Buying Another's Sickness: A person visiting a friend who was near death said to him in jest, "If you pay me this and-so much, I'll buy your sickness." The sick man said, "All right, I'll pay you whatever you're asking for." The sick man recovered at once, and the other fell ill and died (*Sefer Chasidim*).

15. All Must Empathize with the Ill: It is stated in Psalms: "Yet, when they were ill, my clothing was

sackcloth, I kept a fast . . . [Psalms 35:13]. This
teaches us that if one person is in pain, all are
commanded to empathize with his anguish, to be
troubled in his distress, and to pray for him, as it
says, "Far be it from me to sin against God and
refrain from praying for you" [1 Samuel 12:23]
(*Sefer Chasidim*).

16. The Cause of Sickness: Sometimes a person is
tormented with pain and suffering because he
rejoiced in someone's else's misfortune [Pirkei
Avot 4:19], as it says, "He who rejoices over another's misfortune will not go unpunished" [Proverbs
24:17]. Sometimes he is afflicted because he should
have prayed for other people and did not [*Berachot*
12b], and sometimes because he fervently prayed
for something that was not decreed for him. The
Holy One, blessed be He, diverts his attention from
this plea by bringing suffering upon him, so that he
will forget it and instead pray for relief from his
present misery. Sometimes a person is plagued
from pain because he owes money to someone, and
did not pay. Now he is beset by pain so that he will
have to pay the money to doctors [Song of Songs
Rabbah 6:671]. The pain will last until he considers
paying the money he owes. When he pays his debt,
his sickness will depart, so that he will know that
this was the cause of his affliction, and he will be
cleansed for the world-to-come (*Sefer Chasidim*).

THE OBLIGATION
TO HEAL

One who is instrumental in saving one person's life is like one who saves the entire world (*Sanhedrin* 4, 5).

Judaism teaches that the value of human life is so important that it takes precedence over virtually all other considerations. The value that Judaism places on life is aptly summed up in the following rabbinic passage regarding the creation of Adam:

Therefore only a single human being was created in the world to teach that if any person has caused a single soul of Israel to perish, the Bible regards him as if he had caused an entire world to perish; and if any human being saves a single soul of Israel, the Bible regards him as if he had saved an entire world (*Sanhedrin* 37a).

The religious duty to save the life of an endangered person is derived by the talmudic tractate *Sanhedrin* 73a, from the verse "Do not stand idly by the blood of your fellow" (Leviticus 19:16). The Talmud and various Jewish law codes offer specific examples of when a person is required to render assistance to persons in trouble, including cases of a person drowning in a body of water and one who is mauled by wild beasts.

There are quite a number of talmudic citations which support the position that not only allows but requires the patient to seek medical assistance when sick. We are told (*Baba Kamma* 46b) that one who is in pain should go to a physician. Further, in the talmudic tractate *Yoma* 83b we are told that if one is bitten by a snake, one may call a physician even if it means desecrating the Sabbath.

The principle of human medical intervention with regard to preserving and saving a life has brought with it theological debate over the centuries. There were those who believed that an all-powerful God would not allow His creatures to become ill in the first place, unless the illness was meant to be some kind of punishment for a transgression that had been committed. In that view, human intervention using medical procedures was seen as a lack of faith in God. The Karaites, a middle-eighth-century sect, rejected talmudic traditional authority and based themselves on individual interpretation of the biblical teachings. They rejected all forms of human healing, instead relying entirely upon prayer for the healing of the ill. They based their position on a literal reading and interpretation of Exodus 15:26, which reads as follows: "I will put none of the diseases upon you which I have put upon the Egyptians, for I am the Lord your physician." Thus the Karaites taught that God alone was to be sought as the Physician.

This view was rejected by rabbinic authorities,

who often used the text of Exodus 21:19–20 as authorization for a physician to cure the ill: "And if other men quarrel with one another and one smites the other with a stone or with the fist and he dies not, but has to keep in bed . . . he must pay the loss entailed by absence from work and he shall cause him to be thoroughly healed."

A second verse often used by the rabbis to point out God's authorization for humans to heal is Deuteronomy 22:2: "And you shall restore the lost property to him." On the basis of an extra letter in the Hebrew text of this passage, the Talmud asserts that the verse includes the obligation to not only restore a person's property, but also to restore a person to health.

In biblical times, healing was in the hands of God, and the physician's role was that of helper or instrument of God. Numerous references to physicians and men of healing appear throughout the Bible. It is always implied, however, that although a person may administer treatment, God does the healing: "I am the Lord Who heals you" (Exodus 15:26). The name *rofey* (healer) was, therefore, never adopted by ancient Jewish physicians. Hebrew priests had no authority as physicians, but rather acted as health wardens of the Israelite community, charged with enforcing the laws pertaining to social hygiene.

The following rabbinic tale indicates the clear rabbinic assertion that the work of a physician is legitimate, and that physicians work with God as partners in the healing process.

It once happened that Rabbi Ishmael and Rabbi Akiva were strolling in the streets of Jerusalem accompanied by another person. They were met by a sick person. He said to them, "My masters, tell me by what means I may be cured." The sick man asked them, "And who afflicted me?" They replied, "The Holy One, blessed be the One." The sick man responded, "You have entered into a matter that does not pertain to you. God has afflicted, and you seek to cure. Are you not transgressing God's will?"

Rabbi Akiva and Rabbi Ishmael asked him, "What is your occupation?" The sick man answered, "I am a tiller of the soil, and here is the sickle in my hand." They asked him, "Who created the vineyard?" "The Holy Blessed One," he answered. Rabbi Akiva and Rabbi Ishmael said to him, "You enter into a matter that does not pertain to you. God created the vineyard, and you cut fruits from it."

He said to them, "Do you not see the sickle in my hand? If I did not plow, sow, fertilize, and weed, nothing would sprout."

Rabbi Akiva and Rabbi Ishmael said to him, "Foolish man. Just as if one does not weed, fertilize, and plow, the trees will not produce fruit, and if fruit is produced but is not watered or fertilized, it will not live but die, so with regard to the body. Drugs and medicaments are the fertilizers, and the physician is the tiller of the soil" (Midrash Temurrah).

Maimonides, the medieval philosopher, asserts that the biblical obligation related to restoring lost property not only establishes an obligation for the physician to render professional services, but also indicates that the obligation extends to all individuals to restore their fellow human beings to proper health.

Nachmanides also finds that the obligation to heal is inherent in the biblical precept "You shall love your neighbor as yourself" (Leviticus 19:18). In his writings, he declares that the obligation to heal includes not only life-threatening situations, but any situation in which there is pain that may be alleviated.

Despite the many rabbinic rulings favoring the requirement to heal the sick, some views exist that are not in favor of the healing arts. For instance, Abraham ibn Ezra (*Commentary on the Bible*, Exodus 21:19) finds a contradiction between the injunction "And he shall cause to be thoroughly healed" and the account in 2 Chronicles 16:12 of Asa, the king of Judah, who became very sick and "sought not to God, but to the physicians." The commentators ibn Ezra and Nachmanides interpreted the verse to mean that Asa was censured for seeking medical assistance from physicians because he failed to realize that they were only vehicles for divine healing.

THE ROLE AND STATUS
OF THE JEWISH PHYSICIAN

Judaism has always viewed the seeking of medical attention as a moral necessity. Jews are obligated to take care of their bodies and to seek medical care when necessary. However, there is no absolute obligation to study medicine, nor is a person obligated to engage in any specific research designed to advance the knowledge of medicine.

In the Bible, Joseph employed house physicians (Genesis 1:2), and Isaiah the prophet mentions a surgeon or wound-dresser (Isaiah 3:7). Among the Jews, unlike in other primitive nations, the priests did not monopolize the art and science of healing. Moses assigned to the priests the task of supervision in case of contagious diseases. The prophets, however, practiced occasionally the art of healing. Isaiah cured King Hezekiah (2 Kings 20:7) of an inflammation by applying a plaster made of figs, and Elijah brought to life a child apparently dead (1 Kings 17:17–22).

Various opinions in the Talmud point to the fact that calling upon a physician for medical aid was not to be viewed as a failure to rely upon God to restore health: "Whoever is in pain, let that person go to the physician" (Baba Kamma 46b).

We know from various talmudic sources that there were a substantial number of practicing physicians in rabbinic times. The Talmud (Sanhedrin 17b) enumerates ten things that must be in a city where a scholar lives, among them both a physician and a surgeon. Many outstanding Jewish scholars achieved fame as prominent doctors. Interestingly, in the majority of cases, the art of healing was transmitted from father to son. Among the best-known are Mar Samuel, a judge and head of an academy of learning, who is credited with discovering an ointment for curing eye diseases. In the twelfth century, Judah Halevi, a poet and philosopher, also became a highly sought-after doctor in Spain. The twelfth-century philosopher Maimonides, considered by many to be the greatest of all Jewish scholars, wrote numerous medical works and served as the personal physician to the family of Sultan Saladin of Egypt.

The physician, seen as an instrument of God, the ultimate Healer, was held in high esteem: "Honor the physician before need of him. Him also has God apportioned. The skill of a physician shall lift up his head and he shall stand before nobles" (Ecclesiasticus 38).

That the demand upon the skill of physicians was considerable may be adduced from the statute law prohibiting the part-owner of a house from renting his part to a physician on account of the noise and disturbance caused by the visiting patients (*Baba Batra* 21a). The sum total of medical knowledge possessed by the ancient Hebrews cannot be stated definitively, since no ancient medical treatises have been preserved. The Mishneh (*Pesachim* 4, 9) mentions a medical book, *Sefer Refu'ot*, attributed to King Solomon and expurgated by King Hezekiah, and the talmudic tractate *Yoma* 38a cites a treatise on pharmacology known as *Megillat Sammanin*.

The Talmud names two types of doctors: *rofey* (skilled physician) and *rofey umman* (surgeon). Patients in talmudic times visited the physician in his home. For this reason, according to *Baba Batra* 21a, a special regulation was enacted that required anyone renting premises to a doctor to obtain the prior agreement of his neighbors, since the cries and noises of visiting patients might disturb them.

Although it appears that hospitals did not exist in talmudic times, the tractate *Sanhedrin* 78a makes mention of operating rooms, known as *battei shay-ish*, that were required to be walled with marble for cleanliness. There were communal or district physicians whose duties included assessing the character and extent of any physical disability sustained in cases of injury in order to determine the damages. They were also required, as reported in tractate *Makkot* 22b, to judge the degree of physical endurance of a person sentenced to corporal punishment. According to *Baba Kamma* 85a, the victim of an assault could refuse to be treated by a physician coming from a distance, since the physician would not be sufficiently concerned with the welfare of the patient.

Doctors' Fees

It was expected that physicians be adequately remunerated for services rendered. Working free of charge was never suggested because, according to the Talmud, "a physician that did not charge a fee was worth nothing" (*Baba Kamma* 85a). Joseph Caro, in his *Code of Jewish Law*, Yoreh De'ah, Chap. 336, sec. 2, had this to say about doctors' fees:

One must also make mention of the fact that Jewish physicians were known to be particularly sympathetic to the poor and needy. The Talmud (*Taanit*

21b) tells of a doctor named Abba Umana, who, in order not to discourage indigent patients, would hang a box on the wall where anyone could put in, unnoticed, any fee that he could afford for the medical treatment that was provided. We are further told that he refused to take fees from poor students and would always return their money so that they would use it for rehabilitation.

Caro explains that physicians, like rabbis and teachers, were to receive money not for their actual services, but only for the interruption of their time:

A physician may not accept a fee for giving advice to a patient, because in sharing learning and wisdom with his patient, he performs the religious duty of restoring health to a person who has lost it. And just as God performs his services gratuitously, so should a physician. However, a physician may accept payment for the time he spends in visiting a patient, and the trouble he takes to write prescriptions (*Code of Jewish Law*, Yoreh De'ah, Chap. 336, sec. 2).

For ancient physicians, there was no such thing as malpractice insurance. If, in spite of every care, a licensed doctor injured a patient or caused his death, he was not, as among many other peoples, held guilty (*Sanhedrin* 84b). Joseph Caro's *Code of Jewish Law* explains both the responsibilities and the liabilities of a doctor. More lenient than common law, Jewish law does not hold the doctor legally liable for injuring a patient, although he is considered morally accountable. The doctor is, however, liable for the death of a patient through negligence:

> The Torah grants physicians permission to heal. Healing is in fact a religious duty that falls under the category of saving a life.
>
> If a physician withholds treatment when he is able to give it, he is regarded as a murderer, even if there is someone else who can heal a patient, because it may be that in this case it is the special merit of this physician to provide the healing for the patient.
>
> However, a person should not practice medicine unless he is an expert, and there is no one immediately available who is more competent than he. Otherwise, he is regarded as a murderer. If a person gives medical treatment without the permission of a Jewish court [today's equivalent of practicing medicine without a degree or board certification], he is subject to payment of indemnities, even if he is an expert.
>
> If he had the proper credentials but made a mistake in judgment and negligently injured the patient, he is exempt from the laws of man but is held responsible by the laws of heaven. If the doctor causes a death because of negligence, he is exiled according to the laws that deal with a person who killed another accidentally (*Code of Jewish Law*, Yoreh De'ah, Chap. 336, sec. 1).

The *Encyclopedia Judaica* (vol. 11) reports that Jewish physicians had outstanding reputations and practiced throughout the then-known civilized world. A man named Theudas is mentioned in the talmudic tractate *Bechorot* 4:4 as a famous doctor from Alexandria. Emperor Antoninus Pius requested none other than Judah Ha-Nasi, editor of the Mishneh, to supply him from his circle of friends with a physician for his house slaves. The personal physician of Saint Basil was a Jew named Ephraim.

The study of medicine was also included in the curriculum of talmudic schools, and many talmudic scholars were themselves doctors. Most noteworthy among them were Rabbi Ishmael, Rabbi Chanina ben Dosa, Rabbi Chananiah ben Chama, Joseph Ha-Rofey of Gamla, Tobiah Ha-Rofey of Modi'in, and Samuel Bar Abba Ha-Kohen, to whom many remedies and knowledge of the anatomy are attributed. Samuel Bar Abba Ha-Kohen was the personal doctor of the King of Persia.

Asaf Ha-Rofey

One of the most famous early physicians in the history of Jewish medicine is a sixth-century doctor known as Asaf Ha-Rofey (also known as Asaf Ha-Yehudi, Rabbenu Asaf, Asaf ben Berechia). He gave his name to a book on medicine called *Sefer Asaf Ha-Rofey* that circulated in the Middle East. His book constituted a source of information on ancient customs and Jewish medical ethics, as well as ancient Jewish remedies and Hebrew, Aramaic, Persian, Latin, and Greek medical terminology.

The Oath of Asaf's Students

Following is an excerpt from the sermon that Asaf imposed on his students. There are some similarities to the famous Hippocratic Oath of physicians.

> "Take heed that you kill not any man with a root decoction; do not prepare any potion that may cause a woman who has conceived in adultery to miscarry; and do not lust after beautiful women to commit adultery with them; and do not divulge a man's secret that he has confided unto you; and do not be bribed to do injury and harm and do not harden your heart against the poor and the needy; rather have compassion on them and heal them. Do not speak of good as evil nor of evil as good. Do not follow in the ways of sorcerers to enchant by witchcraft and magic to part a man from his beloved or a woman from the husband of her youth. . . . Be mindful of Him at all times and seek Him in truth and righteousness all the days of your life and in all that you do and He will help you in all your undertakings and you shall be happy in the eyes of all men. The peoples will neglect their gods and idols and will yearn to serve the Lord as you do, for they will perceive that they have put their trust in mockery and that they have labored in vain—when they turn to their god he will not help and will not save. And as for you, be strong and let not your hands slacken for you shall be rewarded for your labors. The Lord is with you and when you are with Him and if you keep His covenant and walk in His statutes and cleave to them you shall be as saints in the eyes of all flesh, for they will say 'Happy is the

people that is in such a state, happy is the people whose God is the Lord.'"

And their disciples answered and declared: "All that you have admonished us and commanded us we shall do for it is ordained in the Torah and we will carry it out with all our heart and soul and might; we will do and listen and not deviate nor turn to left or right."

Ben Sira:
The Physician as an Instrument of God

The Jewish attitude toward the physician, and the patient's responsibility to seek medical aid, are described by Ben Sira (Ecclesiasticus 38), who perceived in the physician an instrument of God:

Honor a physician before need of him
Him also has God apportioned
From God a physician gets wisdom
And from a king he shall receive gifts.
The skill of a physician shall lift up his head
And he shall stand before nobles
God brings out medicines from the earth
And let a prudent man not refuse them.
Was not water made sweet with wood
For to acquaint every man with His power?
And He gave man understanding
To glory in His might.
By them does the physician assuage pain
And likewise the apothecary makes a confection,
That His work may not fail
Nor health from among the sons of men.
My son, in sickness be not negligent

Pray unto God, for God will heal.
Flee from iniquity, and from respect of persons
And from all transgressions cleanse your heart.
Offer a sweet savor as a memorial
And fatness estimated according to your substance.
And to the physician also give a place
And he shall not remove, for there is need of him
  likewise,
For there is a time when in his hand is good success.
For he too will supplicate unto God
That God will prosper to him the treatment
And the healing, for the sake of his living.
He that sins against his Maker
Will behave himself proudly against a physician.

The Medical Oath of Maimonides

In modern times, as physicians are about to begin their medical practice, they take an oath. The Hippocratic Oath has for centuries been the standard vow. The Medical Oath of Maimonides is often chosen by Jewish doctors, and is now being used in some medical schools as well. Here is the Medical Oath of Maimonides:

> Your eternal providence has appointed me to watch over the life and health of Your creatures. May the love for my art actuate me at all times, may neither avarice nor miserliness, nor thirst for glory, or for a great reputation engage my mind, for the enemies of truth and philanthropy could easily deceive me and make me forgetful of my lofty aim of doing good to Your children.
>
> May I never see in the patient anything but a fellow creature in pain.

Grant me strength, time, and opportunity always to correct what I have acquired, always to extend its domain, for knowledge is immense and the spirit of man can extend indefinitely to enrich itself daily with new requirements.

Today he can discover his errors of yesterday and tomorrow he can obtain a new light on what he thinks himself sure of today. O God, You have appointed me to watch over the life and death of Your creatures, here I am ready for my vocation and now I turn to my calling.

Maimonides' Physician's Prayer

In addition to the Medical Oath of Maimonides, a most beautiful and moving physician's prayer is attributed to him that contains the ethical standards by which a doctor should conduct his professional life. Here follows Maimonides' Daily Prayer of a Physician:

Almighty God, You have created the human body with infinite wisdom. Ten thousand times ten thousand organs have You combined in it that act unceasingly and harmoniously to preserve the whole in all its beauty—the body, which is the envelope of the mortal soul. They are ever-acting in perfect order, agreement, and accord. Yet, when the frailty of matter or the unbridling of passions deranges this order or interrupts this accord, then forces clash and the body crumbles into the primal dust from which it came, You send to man diseases as beneficent messengers to foretell approaching danger and to urge him to avert it.

You have blessed Your earth, Your rivers, and Your mountains with healing substances; they enable Your creatures to alleviate their sufferings and to heal their illnesses. You have endowed man with the wisdom to relieve the suffering of his brother, to recognize his disorders, to extract the healing substances, to discover their powers and to prepare and to apply them to suit every will. In Your eternal presence You have chosen me to watch over the life and health of Your creatures. I am now about to apply myself to the duties of my profession. Support me, Almighty God, in these great labors that they may benefit mankind, for without Your help not even the least thing will succeed.

Inspire me with love for my art and for Your creatures. Do not allow thirst for profit, ambition for renown and admiration, to interfere with my profession, for these are the enemies of truth and of love for mankind and they can lead astray in the great task of attending to the welfare of Your creatures. Preserve the strength of my body and of my soul that they ever be ready to cheerfully help and support rich and poor, good and bad, enemy as well as friend. In the sufferer let me see only the human being. Illumine my mind that it recognize what presents itself and that it may comprehend what is absent or hidden. Let it not fail to see what is visible, but do not permit it to arrogate to itself the power to see what cannot be seen, for delicate and indefinite are the bounds of the great art of caring for the lives and health of Your creatures. Let me never be absent-minded. May no strange thoughts divert my attention at the bedside of the sick, or disturb my mind in its silent labors, for great and sacred are the thoughtful deliberations required to preserve the lives and health of Your creatures.

Grant that my patients have confidence in me and my art and follow my directions and my counsel. Remove from their midst all charlatans, and the whole host of officious relatives and know-all nurses, cruel people who arrogantly frustrate the wisest purposes of our art and often lead Your creatures to their death.

Should those who are wiser than I wish to improve and instruct me, let my soul gratefully follow their guidance; for vast is the extent of our art. Should conceited fools, however, censure me, then let love for my profession steel me against them, so that I remain steadfast without regard for age, for reputation, or for honor, because surrender would bring to Your creatures sickness and death.

Imbue my soul with gentleness and calmness when older colleagues, proud of their age, wish to displace me or to scorn me or disdainfully to teach me. May even this be of advantage to me, for they know many things of which I am ignorant, but let not their arrogance give me pain. For they are old and old age is not master of the passions. I also hope to attain old age upon this earth, before You, Almighty God! Let me be contented in everything except in the great science of my profession. Never allow the thought to arise in me that I have attained to sufficient knowledge, but vouchsafe to me the strength, the leisure, and the ambition ever to extend my knowledge. For art is great, but the mind is ever-expanding. Almighty God! You have chosen me in Your mercy to watch over the life and death of Your creatures. I now apply myself to my profession. Support me in this great task so that it may benefit mankind, for without Your help not even the least thing will succeed.

NOTABLE QUOTATIONS ON PHYSICIANS

1. The Customs of Abba the Therapeutic Blood-Letter: Abba the Therapeutic Blood-Letter would receive greetings of peace every day from the Torah School in the Sky. Abaye would receive similar greetings, but only once a week, before the Sabbath. Rava, too, would get similar well-wishes, but only once a year before Yom Kippur. Abaye was troubled by the particular distinction shown to Abba the Blood-Letter. He was told: "You have not achieved what Abba has achieved." And what were these things that Abba the Blood-Letter did? When he was performing his operations, he would separate the men from the women. Furthermore, he had a special gown with slits in it, through which he would put the bleeding instrument. Whenever a woman would come for treatment, he would have her wear this gown, so that he would not have to unnecessarily expose her body. In addition, he had a place—away from public view—where people could pay their fees. Whoever could pay would pay there, and whoever could not would not be embarrassed.

When he would see a sage who could not afford to pay, he would say: "Take this money as a loan and get your strength back."

One day, Abaye sent two sages to investigate the situation. He gave them seats, gave them food and drink, and at night gave them wool mattresses to sleep on. In the morning they rolled up the mattresses and took them with them. They went out to the market, where they encountered him. They said: "How much would you say these are worth, sir?" He said: "They are worth such-and-such." They said: "Maybe they are worth more." He said: "That is how much I paid for them." They said to him: "They are yours. We took them. Forgive us, but what did you suspect?" He said: "I assumed that the rabbis were involved in the *mitzvah* of redeeming some captives but were embarrassed to ask for money." They said: "Now you should take them back, sir." He said: "From the moment you took them, I no longer considered them mine. As far as I was concerned, they belonged to *tzedakah*" (*Taanit* 21b–22a).

2. No Charge for Healing: A person should not charge a fee for healing [*Nedarim* 37a]. He may tell the patient, "Pay me for my expenses"—in other words, "Reimburse me for my time and trouble." But he should not receive a fee for the cure, only for his trouble and expenses. If someone says, "Just tell me what to do," the doctor should not charge anything [merely for giving advice] (*Sefer Chasidim*).

3. The Gentile Doctor and a Jew: When a gentile doctor heals a Jew, the Jew should pay him. If he does not, Heaven will grant the gentile a rich reward in this world, and a portion of the Jew's share in the world-to-come will be taken from him and given to the gentile. Thus, the gentile will be rewarded both in this world and in the world-to-come (*Sefer Chasidim*).

MEDICINE, DISEASES, AND REMEDIES

Eating vegetables is recommended for maintaining good health (*Berachot* 40a).

IN THE BIBLE

The main source of information related to ancient medicine is the Bible. No ancient Hebrew medical documents exist; the Talmud (*Berachot* 10b, *Pesachim* 56a) reports that King Hezekiah canceled the "Medical Book" and that a scroll on pharmacology was lost. The Israelites were likely influenced in their concepts of medicine by the surrounding peoples of the ancient Near East. The Bible says almost nothing about medical practice itself. The cures performed by the prophets Elijah and Elisha are presented as miraculous wonder stories.

As mentioned earlier in this volume, healing in ancient time was left primarily in God's hands. As the Israelites set out from Egypt toward the Sea of Reeds, God says: "If you will listen to the Lord your God and keep all of His laws, then I will not bring

upon you any of the diseases that I brought upon
the Egyptians, for I the Lord am your Healer"
(Exodus 15:26). Theologically speaking, this statement becomes an important one, for it connects the
keeping of God's laws with the absence of disease,
seeming to imply that good behavior and following
God's commandments will help a person stay
disease-free.

The specialness of biblical medicine lies in its
many regulations for social hygiene, which continue to be remarkable for their insightfulness
even by today's standards. About one-third of all
the religious obligations (mitzvot) in the Five Books
of Moses are of a medical nature. These include
commandments related to the suppression of pros-
titution; frequent washing of the body; skin care;
dietary and sanitary regulations; rules for sexual
life; and isolation and quarantine when struck
with a contagious disease. For instance, Numbers
19:7–16 enumerates the laws related to one who
has come into contact with a corpse. Numbers
20:22–24 describes the requirement to cleanse the
garments, weapons, and utensils of soldiers re-
turning to camp after a battle in order to prevent
infectious diseases. The danger of infectious bowel
diseases (possibly picked up during contact with
the enemy) and the cleansing of the camp is described in these verses from Deuteronomy 23:13–
14.

You shall have a place also without the camp,
whither you shall go forth abroad. And you shall
have a paddle among your weapons, and it shall be,

when you sit down abroad, you shall dig therewith and shall turn back and cover that which comes from you.

BIBLICAL DISEASES

Numerous diseases are mentioned throughout the Bible. Here is a listing of some of them: *shachefet* (phthisis) in Leviticus 26:16; *afolim* (leishmaniasis) in Deuteronomy 28:27; *yerakon* (ikterus) in Deuteronomy 28:22; *zav* (gonorrhea) in Leviticus 15; *shivron motnayim* (lumbago) in Ezekiel 21:11; *nofel vegalui aynayim* (epilepsy) in Numbers 24:4; *rekav atzamot* (osteomyelitis) in Proverbs 14:13. It has been conjectured that Isaac's dimness of sight (Genesis 48:10) may have been the result of cataracts. Other diseases mentioned in the Bible include hydrocele (Leviticus 22:22), harelip (Deuteronomy 23:2), and mental disturbances like madness (Deuteronomy 28:28). Finally, various forms of skin disease are referred to in Deuteronomy 28:27: "God will smite you with the boil of Egypt, and with the emerods, and with the scab and itch, whereof you cannot be healed."

Leprosy: The Most Dreaded Biblical Disease

The most dreaded of all biblical diseases is *tzara'at*, usually translated as leprosy but more likely referring to a number of skin ailments, many of which were curable. (True leprosy is now referred to as

Hansen's disease, after the nineteenth-century Norwegian physician who identified the microorganism that causes it.) The Bible treats the leper as an outcast from both the physical and the spiritual community. It has been said that the twentieth-century version of leprosy is AIDS, the major difference being that AIDS cannot yet be cured, whereas certain forms of biblical leprosy were curable. Whereas in biblical times almost all sicknesses and maladies were cared for by ordinary healers, the only sickness treated by the *kohen*—the Jewish priest—is leprosy. There is good reason for this. Because leprosy was the most terrifying and frightening disease of that time, the people's first reaction was to bar the leper from the camp because he was contagious. Therefore, the Bible made it the responsibility of the *kohen*, the spiritual head of the community, to quarantine the leper if necessary, but, more importantly, to always maintain a relationship with him and to ultimately bring him back when he was totally healed.

If leprosy was viewed as a plague, the expression of God's anger for a misdeed, it was natural to inquire what sin evoked this horrendous punishment. Long before the birth of psychosomatic medicine, the rabbis sensed that physical defects were often rooted in spiritual shortcomings. The ancient rabbinic authorities derived from leprosy a moral lesson. Homiletically interpreting the word *metzora* (leper) as connected with the words *motzei shem ra* (a person guilty of slander or libel), they regarded leprosy primarily as a divine punishment for this evil, an interpretation that is supported historically by Miriam's punishment of leprosy for her slander of Moses in Numbers 12:1–15. According to the Talmud, among other sins that bring leprosy as retribution are "the shedding of blood, taking oaths in vain, incest, arrogance, robbery, and envy." (*Arachin* 16a).

The Role of the Priest

The thirteenth and fourteenth chapters of Leviticus contain the basic laws related to leprosy, its diagnosis and ritual, the important role of the priest, and the prescribed ritual for the healed leper. In contrast to his pagan counterpart, who often resorted to various forms of magic and incantation, the *kohen* did not practice magic and was involved only in the contagious skin diseases enumerated in Leviticus. He was not a healer per se, but rather a type of health official who saw to it that the leper was properly quarantined.

The initial problem faced by the priest was to determine whether the sufferer had acute leprosy (indicated by a whitish discoloration of the body hair in the infected areas of the skin), or some less acute ailment that would heal. The priest was called in to inspect the affliction; if leprosy was suspected, the priest imposed a seven-day quarantine. At the end of this period the afflicted was again examined, and if no further degeneration was apparent, he was isolated for one additional week, after which he was pronounced healed. If the skin rash continued to spread, the person was considered to have acute leprosy and was declared impure indefinitely. It was the responsibility of those afflicted with these skin diseases to both pray and fast in order to win God's healing.

The rites ordained for the purification of a person who had suffered from leprosy are among the most elaborate in the priestly laws. The prescribed ritual for the healed leper involved three separate ceremonies. On the first day (Leviticus 14:2–8), a ritual was performed by the priest outside the camp from which the leper was banished. Cedar wood, crimson cloth, and a live bird were dipped into an earthen vessel containing a mixture of fresh water and the blood of a second bird. Both blood and fresh water were known for their strong powers of purification in biblical times. The leper (or leprous house) was sprinkled with this mixture seven times, after which the live bird was set free. (The live bird symbolically carried with it the defilement, much like the ritual of the scapegoat in Leviticus, where a goat was sent into the wilderness symbolically carrying the sins of all the Israelites). The leper was then admitted into the camp after washing his clothes, shaving, and bathing. On the seventh day, the leper was allowed into his home after shaving, laundering his clothes, and bathing again. On the eighth day, the leper brought to the sanctuary oil and sheep for various sacrificial offerings. The purpose of this altar ritual was sanctificatory, allowing the leper return to society as a full-working member of the Israelite community.

BIBLICAL REMEDIES

In the main, biblical remedies and treatments are all of a rational character and do not involve magical incantations. One exception was the brass serpent that was employed to heal dangerous snake-bites (Numbers 21:9) but, we are told (2 Kings 18:4), was destroyed by King Hezekiah. Biblical medicinal therapy consisted of washing the body, using oils and balsams, bandages for bone fractures and wounds, and bathing in therapeutic waters (2 Kings 5:10), especially in the case of skin diseases. Among the biblical medicaments mentioned by name are myrrh, sweet cinnamon, assia, galbanum, niter, and the mandrake. People in biblical times also were aware of mouth-to-mouth resuscitation; the prophets Elijah and Elisha are described as knowing how to perform it in order to save lives (1 Kings 17:22, 2 Kings 4:34–35).

1 Samuel 16 describes the beneficial effect of music on King Saul, who was suffering from melancholia. Some have contended that the method employed by Moses to sweeten the undrinkable bitter waters of Marah (Exodus 15:22–25) was an early instance of desalination.

IN THE TALMUD

Etiology

Talmudic scholars had many opportunities to observe and diagnose disease, based on their interest in the ritual fitness of animals and the purity of community members. Detailed descriptions of various body parts are given in the Talmud, particularly in tractate *Chullin*, which deals with the fitness of animals for food and similar subjects. *Chullin* places special emphasis on types of muscles, which, it notes, change their form when in motion. Tendons, glands, cartilage, and intestines are also scrutinized. It is interesting to note (*Chullin* 59a) Rabbi Chisdai's observation that the *psoas* (internal muscle of the loin) in all permissible animals (i.e., kosher animals that chew their cud and have split hooves) has two accessory muscles whose respective fibers run longitudinally and transversely, while the *psoas* of forbidden (i.e., non-kosher) animals does not have the extra muscles.

The structure of the esophagus, larynx, and trachea is traced, as is the course of the alimentary canal and the gastrointestinal tract. Organs described include the liver and diaphragm, spleen and kidneys, lungs, pleura, heart, spinal cord, and brain. A most radical opinion for this time was expressed by Rav (Abba Areka of the third century c.e.) when he asserted that the aorta contains blood, not air (*Chullin* 45b). The mystical book known as the *Zohar* describes the skull as containing three cavities in which the brain is lodged, and states that thirty-two paths extend from the brain to various parts of the body.

The following is a brief summary of rabbinic findings (up to the thirteenth century c.e.) related to knowledge of the body, the relationship of physical attributes to personality, and disease.

1. Paleness of Body: Disturbances of the circulatory system were recognized by paleness of the body (*Yevamot* 64b).

2. The Eye: Rabbis were able to recognize the macula of the cornea, keratitis, and detached retina (*Bechorot* 88a).

3. Diphtheria: Diphtheria as an epidemic disease that causes painful death through strangulation was recognized by Rabbi Ishmael (*Yevamot* 64a).

4. Hemophilia: The pathology of hemophilia as a lack of viscosity in the blood that prevents blood clotting, thus prohibiting the circumcision of an infant hemophiliac, was known in rabbinic times (*Chullin* 47b).

5. Diseases Caused by Worms: Liver, lung, kidney, and stomach diseases caused by worms were known in rabbinic times (*Chullin* 48a, *Shabbat* 109b, *Gittin* 70a).

6. Digestive Disturbances: Lack of fluids was thought to lead to digestive disturbances (*Shabbat* 41a).

7. Fear and the Pulse Rate: Fear hastens a person's rate (*Sanhedrin* 100b).

8. The Danger of Falling: Falling from heights may cause fatal internal injury (*Chullin* 42a).

9. Spinal Cord Injury: Injury to the spinal cord causes paralysis (*Chullin* 51a).

10. Infectious Diseases: Animals and insects are carriers of infectious diseases (*Ketubot* 77a).

11. Contaminated Water: Contaminated water may make a person ill (*Avodah Zarah* 30a).

12. The Importance of Sleep: Sleep is like food and medicine to the sick (*Pirkei de Rabbi Eliezer*, p. 12).

13. The Effects of Blindness: When sight is lost, the other senses become keener (*Gittin* 23).

14. Speech: Abnormalities may affect speech. A man may have a thin, feminine voice, and a woman a deep, masculine one (*Yevamot* 10, 6, 7).

15. The Glands: Although all of the glands derive their material from the same source, each gland secretes a fluid peculiar to itself (Numbers Rabbah 15).

16. Tooth Structure: The structure of the teeth differs in herbivorous and carnivorous animals (*Chullin* 59).

17. Digestion in the Animal Kingdom: Birds digest their food rapidly, dogs more slowly (*Shabbat* 82a).

18. Reasoning Faculties: The reasoning faculties are lodged in the brain (*Yevamot* 9a).

19. The Structure of the Heart: The heart is composed of two ventricles, the right one being larger than the left, and is situated to the left of the median line. Each lung has five lobes, and the aorta contains blood. (*Chullin* 45b, 47a).

20. Condition of the Heart: The condition of the heart changes from hour to hour (*Aggadah Bereshit* 2).

21. The Gullet: The gullet has two skins; the outer one is red and the inner one is white (*Chullin* 43).

22. The Indestructible Coccyx: A small bone at the base of the spine called *luz* ("ox coccygis"—the coccyx] is the only part of the human body that is indestructible, and the one from which resurrection will start (Midrash Ecclesiastes, 114, 3).

23. The Liver: When the liver is excited, the gall pours a drop over it, and quiets it (*Berachot* 61b).

24. The Cerebral "Bag": The "bag" in which the cerebrum lies is essential for life (*Chullin* 45a).

25. A Perforated Windpipe: A reed tube was inserted in the perforated windpipe of a lamb, and it recovered (*Chullin* 57b).

26. Glands: Two bean-like glands lie at the mouth of the skull (*Chullin* 45a).

27. The Strongest Hip: The right hip is usually the stronger one (*Chullin* 91a).

28. The Right Index Finger: The index finger of the right hand is usually the most dexterous (*Sifra Leviticus* 3, 3).

29. Tall People: Tall men are usually slower of perception—first, because their chests are narrow, which diminishes the capacity for blood and weakens the action of the brain; second, because it requires a longer time for the heart and the brain to cooperate (*Sefer Shaashu'im* 2).

30. The Bladder: It is difficult for the bladder to discharge its urine when it is too full because its opening consists entirely of fibers, and when it become overladen, the fibers contract and close up the passage (*Sefer Shaashu'im* 9).

31. The Stomach: The stomach has three kinds of fibers—one stretched lengthwise to receive the food, another placed diagonally to retain the food until it is digested, and the third stretched across the width of the stomach to expel the food when digested. There are six intestines: three upper ones of a delicate nature, and three lower ones of a coarser nature. The intestine adjacent to the liver is made of convolutions, so as to detain the food long enough for the liver to absorb the essence of the food. The liver, incidentally, absorbs this not through any opening in the intestines, but by some wonderful energy like that by which the magnet attracts iron (*Sefer Shaashu'im* 9).

32. The Kidneys: The kidneys are receptacles for the blood which is not assimilated into the body. In the breasts of women, blood is assimilated into milk (*Sefer Shaashu'im* 8, 9).

33. Physical Attributes and Personality Traits: One whose face is flushed is hasty and untruthful. One whose eyes are sunken and quick of glance is both deceitful and resourceful. One whose eyebrows are hairy is a bore and of morose disposition. One with a pointed nose and large nostrils is quarrelsome. One with a round forehead is irritable. Thick lips are also a sign of bad temper. Large ears are proof of foolishness. A short neck is evidence of deceit and envy. A large belly generally goes with an abundance of stupidity. Narrow shoulders bespeak narrow-mindedness. A small palm is an indication of a small mind. All tall men are fools (*Sefer Shaashu'im* 2, 1).

34. Optic Nerves: Of all the nerves in the body, the optic nerves are the only ones that are hollow, to allow the power of light to pass through them from the brain to the retina (*Sefer Shaashu'im* 9, 1).

35. The Teeth: Teeth come from the surplus of hard food, and their growth is enhanced if the milk the child drinks is hot. The warmer the milk, the sooner the teeth will appear. Children are not normally born with teeth, because they do not need them while they are sucklings. The incisors appear before the canines and molars, as they come from softer matter, and the molars arrive only when the child begins to eat harder food. The upper molars, being suspended, have three roots each to hold them fast, while the lower ones have only two roots. The milk teeth, coming from softer food, are afterward replaced by the permanent teeth, which come from the harder food that the older child eats. In old age, the teeth fall out because they dry up and wither like plants (*Sefer Shaashu'im* 9).

36. The Neck: The neck serves two purposes: One to cool the vapors issuing from the heart before they reach the brain, the other to make the human voice audible. That is why the windpipe is made of cartilage—neither soft like flesh nor hard like bone. To make the vibrations of the air audible, they must pass through a medium that is neither too soft nor too hard. That is why when the wind blows against water or rocks, it produces no sound, but when it blows against trees or reeds, it becomes audible (*Sefer Shaashu'im* 9, 5).

37. The Effect of Grief on the Body: Grief breaks the body (*Berachot* 58).

38. Dropsy and Gout: Dropsy and gout may be caused by suppressing urine (*Berachot* 25a).

39. Intestinal Problems of Priests: Because the priests continually walked barefoot on the stone pavement of the Temple, they were subject to intestinal troubles (Jerusalem Talmud *Shekalim* 5).

40. Abdominal Problems: Abdominal troubles cause failing of the eyes and palpitation of the heart (*Nedarim* 22a).

41. Medical Advice for an Invalid: An invalid should not drink cold water (*Yalkut Shimoni, Acharei Mot*).

42. Nose and Ear Discharge: A slight discharge from the nose and ears is normal; but, if heavy, this is not healthy (*Baba Metzia* 107a).

43. Epilepsy: Susceptibility to epilepsy is hereditary (*Baba Metzia* 80a).

44. Diarrhea: Diarrhea may be caused by extreme fright (Psalms 29, 9).

45. Medical Problems from Overheating: The exertion of climbing can lead to a person becoming overcome by heat. Animals, too, may suffer from heat prostration (*Baba Metzia* 6, 3).

46. Poison in the Bloodstream: Poison can enter one's bloodstream through a scratch on the skin (*Tosefta Terumot* 7, 14).

47. Disease and the Change of Seasons: Disease is more prevalent at the change of seasons (Jerusalem Talmud *Yevamot* 15, 14).

48. Medical Problems Resulting from Anger: Anger causes stomach problems . . . every quick-tempered, irritable person is a fool (Ecclesiastes Rabbah 11, 10).

49. The Importance of Saliva: Swallowing a piece of dry bread without its being softened by saliva in the mouth may cause a wound in the entrails (Exodus Rabbah 24).

50. Roots and Impotence: Certain root drinks cause impotence (*Tosefta Yevamot* 8, 4).

51. Fever and the Seasons: Fever is more severe in the winter than in the summer (*Yoma* 29a).

52. The Properties of Dead Flesh: Dead flesh does not feel the knife (*Shabbat* 13b).

53. Skin Over a Fracture: The skin over a fracture retains the pus of a broken bone (*Chullin* 77a).

54. The Air and Disease: All diseases have their origin in the air (*Baba Metzia* 107b).

55. Skin Disease: Skin disease will develop if bleeding is neglected (*Bechorot* 44b).

56. Sickness and Blood: All sicknesses have their effect on the patient's blood (*Baba Batra* 58b).

57. Advice for Blood Transfusions: One should not give a blood transfusion after having eaten fish, fowl, or salted meat (*Nedarim* 54b).

58. Blows and Blood Clots: A blow, though it may not cause bleeding, may cause a blood clot (*Shabbat* 107b).

59. Bleeding: There are families whose members bleed little when wounded, and others who bleed profusely (*Yevamot* 64a).

60. The Importance of Blood: A person cannot live with less than a *revi'it* [approximately 108 cubic centimeters] of blood in the body (*Sotah* 5a, *Chullin* 51a).

61. Blood, Anemia, and Leprosy: If the white corpuscles of the blood outnumber the red, the person is anemic and susceptible to all sicknesses. If the red corpuscles outnumber the white, that person is prone to leprosy and similar plagues (*Tanchuma Leviticus* 6).

62. Blood Type and Heredity: Blood types are hereditary (*Niddah* 64).

63. One Property of Hair: Each hair has its own "well" from which it "drinks." When the well goes dry, the hair does likewise (*Tanchuma Tazria*).

64. Nails: Nails grow only on parts of the body that have bones (*Niddah* 49).

65. Hair-Cutting and Recovery: Hair-cutting retards a patient's convalescence (*Berachot* 57).

66. Fright and Its Effects on Hair: Extreme fright may cause a person's hair to fall out, and may lead to permanent baldness (Exodus Rabbah 24).

67. The Eyeball and Sight: A person sees through the black, not the white, part of the eyeball. This refers to the darkest part in the center of the black (Leviticus Rabbah 31).

68. Body Fluids: Although there are several sources of secretions in the human head very close to each other, each is different. The fluid of the eyes is salty, the ear fluid is oily, the nose fluid has an offensive odor, and the mouth fluid is sweet (Numbers Rabbah 18).

69. Bright Light and Blindness: Sudden blindness may be caused by very bright light (*Gittin* 69a).

70. The Therapeutic Value of Sneezing: The object of sneezing is to free the brain from certain injurious fluids (*Sefer Shaashu'im* 10).

71. Excessive Noise and Deafness: Blowing a horn into someone's ear may deafen that person (*Baba Kamma* 18a).

72. Oil and the Ear: Natural oil in the ears saves a person from dying at loud, penetrating noises, because the oil deadens the sound and makes it bearable (Numbers Rabbah 18).

73. Teeth and Good Health: The health of the body depends on the teeth (*Yalkut Shimoni*, Song of Songs 988).

74. Barrenness: Certain drugs may cause barrenness (*Yevamot* 65b).

75. Menstruation: Excitement prevents regular menstruation (*Niddah* 4, 7).

76. The Pain of Twins: When one of a set of twins has a headache, the other feels the pain as well (Song of Songs Rabbah 5, 2).

77. Circumcision: A weak, sickly infant or one whose blood is not normal is not permitted to be circumcised until he is sufficiently strong to withstand the operation (*Shabbat* 134, 137).

78. The Healing Power of Sleep: Sleep is the best medicine. It strengthens the natural forces and diminishes the injurious fluids (*Sefer Shaashu'im* 9).

79. Excessive Sleep: Too much sleep is inadvisable (*Gittin* 70).

80. Medical Advice for Sleeping: Eight hours of sleep, terminating at dawn, is ideal. One should sleep neither on one's face nor on one's back, but should accustom oneself to sleep first on the left side, and the rest of the night on the right. After eating, one should wait three or four hours before retiring for the night (Maimonides, *Hilchot De'ot*, 4:4, 5).

81. Gout and Arthritis: Gout and arthritis may come from sleeping in a bed that is too short (Pirkei Rabbeinu HaKodesh 3).

82. Antitoxins: The use of antitoxins derived from an infected animal was advocated by Rabbi Ishmael, who prescribed the lobe of a rabid dog's liver as a cure for one bitten by a rabid dog (*Yoma* 84).

83. Remedy for a Sore Throat: A sore throat should be lubricated with olive oil (*Berachot* 36).

84. The Danger of Excessive Sitting: One should not sit too much, for sitting affects the abdominal region. One should not stand too much, for standing affects the heart (*Ketubot* 111a, b).

85. The Healing Power of the Sun: Basking in the sun is good for a wound (Genesis Rabbah 8).

86. Fish and the Eyes: Eating fish is healthy for the eyes (*Nedarim* 54b).

87. Cleaning the Teeth: Scraping is a means of cleaning the teeth (*Kiddushin* 24b).

88. Water Therapy: Better than all the eye salves is a drop of cold water in the eye in the morning and bathing hands and feet with warm water in the evening (*Shabbat* 108b).

89. Walking and Sleeping: A mile's walk or a little sleep counteracts the effect of wine (*Sanhedrin* 22b).

90. Advice for Healing a Fracture: The healing of fractures is aided by splints placed around them (*Shabbat* 53a).

91. Advice on Medicine: It is not wise to accustom oneself to taking medicines, as they will eventually lose their potency (*Pesachim* 113a).

REMEDIES AND TREATMENT FOR DISEASE

A variety of medicines were mentioned throughout the Talmud, including various powders, medicated drinks, balsams, bandages, compresses, and herbs. The following is a cross-section of rabbinic treatments and remedies that were prevalent in bygone years.

1. Meat and Eggs: Meat and eggs were considered to be the most nourishing foods (*Berachot* 44b).

2. Fried or Fatty Foods: Fried foods or foods containing fat are difficult to digest (*Berachot* 57b).

3. Vegetables: Eating vegetables throughout the year and drinking fresh water are highly recommended for maintaining good health (*Berachot* 40a, 57b).

4. Mineral Water and the Skin: Bathing with mineral water is excellent therapy for a variety of skin ailments (*Shabbat* 40a, 109a).

5. Herbs for Constipation: Certain kinds of herbs are good for constipation, and, in serious cases, purges are recommended, except for pregnant women (*Pesachim* 42b).

6. Opium as an Analgetic: The use of opium as an analgetic and hypnotic drug was known, and rabbinic warning was given against overdosing (Jerusalem Talmud, *Avodah Zarah* 2:2, 40d).

7. Salts and Poisons: Certain poisons can be neutralized with salt (Jerusalem Talmud *Terumot* 8, 46).

ANCIENT
FOLK REMEDIES

Five things were said of garlic: It is filling, it keeps the body warm, it brightens the face, it increases semen, and it kills parasites in the bowels (*Baba Kamma* 82).

Although part of ancient medicine was indeed scientific, much of it consisted of a combination of science, superstition, and folklore. Supernatural forces were often considered as causes of illness, and remedies often included incantations accompanied by various strange rites and rituals. The following are some rabbinic passages containing remedies that belong to the category of folk medicine.

1. Remedy for a Fever: Abaye said: "My mother told me that for a daily fever one should take a new *zuz* coin, go to a salt deposit, take the *zuz*'s weight in salt, and tie the salt inside the collar of his shirt with a band of twined strands of wool. If this remedy does not help, the patient should sit at a crossroads, and when he sees a large ant carrying something, he should take it, put it into a brass tube, close the tube's openings with lead, and seal it with sixty seals. He should then shake it, lift it on his back, and say to it, 'Your burden be upon me, and my burden be upon you.' If this remedy does not help, he should take a new jar, small in size, go to the river, and say to it, 'River, O river, lend me a jarful of water for a guest who happens to be visiting me.' He should circle the jar seven times about his head, then pour its water behind his back and say to it, 'River, O river, take back the water you gave me, for the guest who visited me came for a day and left the same day'" (*Shabbat* 66b).

2. Remedy for Tertian Fever: Rabbi Huna said: "As a remedy for tertian fever, one should procure seven prickles from seven date palms, seven chips from seven beams, seven pegs from seven bridges, seven handfuls of ash from seven ovens, seven pinches of earth from seven graves, seven bits of pitch from seven ships, seven seeds of cumin, and seven hairs from the beard of an old dog, and tie them inside the collar of his shirt with a band of twined strands of wool" (*Shabbat* 67a).

3. Remedy for Fever Accompanied by Shivering: Rabbi Yochanan said: "For fever accompanied by shivering, one should take a knife made entirely of iron, go to a place where there is a thornbush, and tie to it bands of twined strands of wool. On the first day, he should make a slight notch in the bush and say, 'The angel of the Lord appeared unto him. . . .' And Moses said: '. . . I will turn aside now . . . and see why the bush is not burnt'" [Exodus 3:2–3].

"On the following day, he should make another

small notch and say, 'When the Lord saw that he turned aside to see' [Exodus 3:4]. The next day, he should make a third small notch and say, 'Do not draw near' [Exodus 3:5]. And when the fever has stopped, he should bend the bush and then cut it down as he says, 'Thornbush, O thornbush, not because you are higher than all other trees in the field did the Holy One have His presence abide upon you, but He had His presence abide upon you because you are lower than all other trees in the field. And even as the fire fled Chananiah, Mishael, and Azariah when it saw them, so may the fire that sees so-and-so, son of so-and-so flee from him'" (*Shabbat* 67a).

4. Remedy for a Rash: For a rash, one should say, "Bazbaziah, Masmasiah, Kaskasiah, Sharlai, and Amarlai"—these are the angels who were sent out from the land of Sodom to heal those smitten with a rash—"Bazakh, Bazikh, Bazbazikh, Masmassikh, Kammon, Kamikh, your color is to remain what it is now, your color is to remain what it is now. Your place is to be confined to where it is now. Your place is to be confined to where it is now. Like one whose seed is locked up, or like a mule that is not fruitful and cannot increase, so may your seed not be fruitful or increase in the body of so-and-so, son of so-and-so" (*Shabbat* 67a).

5. Remedy for Epilepsy: Against epilepsy, one should say, "A sword drawn, a sling stretched, its name is not Yukhav—'sickness and pain'" (*Shabbat* 67a).

6. Remedy for Depression: If a person is seized by depression, what is the way to heal him? Red meat broiled over coals, and diluted wine (*Gittin* 67b).

7. Another Remedy for a Fever: Abaye said: "My mother told me that the remedy for a fever on the first day is to drink a small pitcher of water. If the fever persists for two days, to let blood; if three days, to eat red meat broiled over coals and drink diluted wine. For continuing fever, a person should get a black hen, tear it lengthwise and crosswise, shave the middle of its head, put the hen on its head, and leave it there till it sticks fast. Then he should go down to the river, stand in the water up to his neck until he is faint, and then take a dip and come up.

"For fever, one should eat red meat broiled over coals and diluted wine. For a chill, one should eat fat meat broiled over coals and drink undiluted wine" (*Gittin* 67b).

8. Remedy for Blood Rushing to One's head: For blood rushing to the head, one should take the bark of a box tree, a willow, and myrtle, an olive tree, a sea willow, and a cynodon, and boil them together. Then one should pour three hundred cups [of the concoction] on one side of his head and three hundred cups on the other side. If this remedy does not help, one should take white roses, all of whose leaves are on one side of the stem, boil them, and pour sixty cups of the boiled roses on one side of the head and sixty cups on the other side of his head (*Gittin* 68b).

9. Remedy for a Migraine Headache: For a migraine, one should take a woodcock and cut its throat with a white silver coin over the side of the head where the pain is concentrated, taking care that the blood does not blind his eyes. Then he should hang the bird on his doorpost, so that he can rub against it when he comes in and when he exits (*Gittin* 69a).

10. Remedy for Cataracts: For a cataract, one should take a seven-hued scorpion, dry it in the shade, and mix two parts of ground kohl to one part of ground scorpion; then, with a paintbrush, apply three drops to each eye—no more, lest the eye burst (*Gittin* 69a).

11. Remedies for Night and Day Blindness: For night blindness, a person should take a rope made of wool and with it tie one of his own legs to the leg of a dog, and children should rattle potsherds behind him, saying, "Old dog, stupid cock." He should collect seven pieces of raw meat from seven houses, place them in a door socket, and then have the dog eat them over the ash pit of the town. After that, he should untie the rope, and people should say to him, "Blindness of so-and-so, son of so-and-so, let go of so-and-so, son of so-and-so, and instead seize the pupils of the dog's eyes."

For day blindness, a person should take seven milts from the insides of animals and roast them over a blood-letter's shard. While the blind man sits inside the house, another man should sit outside, and the blind man should say to him, "Give me something to eat." The sighted man should then reply, "Take and eat." After the blind man has eaten, he should then break the shard. Otherwise, the blindness will come back (*Gittin* 69a).

12. How to Stop a Nosebleed: To stop a nosebleed, a man should call a priest whose name is Levi and write "Levi" backward, or else call any other man and write backward, "I am Papi Shila bar Sumki," or else write "the taste of the bucket in water of blemish."

If this remedy does not work, one should take clover roots, the rope of an old bed, papyrus, saffron, and the red part of a palm branch, and burn them all together. Then he should take a fleece of wool, twine it into wicks, steep the wicks in vinegar, roll them in ashes, and put them into his nostrils. If this remedy does not help, he should look for a water channel running from east to west, stand alongside it, pick up some clay from under his left foot with his right hand and from under his right foot with his left hand, twine two more fleeces of wool into wicks, rub the wicks in clay, and put them into his nostrils. If this remedy does not help either, he should sit under a drainpipe and have people bring water, and sprinkle it over him as they say, "Even as these waters will stop, so shall the blood of so-and-so, son of so-and-so stop" (*Gittin* 69a).

13. How to Stop Bleeding from the Mouth: To stop bleeding from the mouth, the blood should be tested by means of a wheaten straw. If the straw is softened, the blood comes from the lung, and there is a remedy for that. If the straw is not softened, the blood comes from the liver, and there is no remedy for that.

If the blood comes from the lung, what is the remedy? He should take seven fistfuls of jujube berry, three fistfuls of lentils, a fistful of cumin, a fistful of string, and a quantity equal to all these of the ileum of a firstborn animal. Then he should cook the mixture and eat it, washing it down with strong beer made during the month of Tevet (*Gittin* 69a).

14. Remedy for a Toothache: For a toothache, Rabbah bar R. Chuna said: "A man should take a whole head of garlic, grind it with oil and salt, and apply it with his thumbnail to the side where the tooth aches. He must put a rim of dough around it, thus taking care that it does not touch his flesh, as it may cause leprosy" (*Gittin* 69a).

15. Remedy for Catarrh in the Head: For a catarrh in the head, one should take gum ammoniac equal to the size of a pistachio nut, galbanum equal to the size of a walnut, honeycake, a spoonful of white honey, and a *mahozan natla* (i.e., a small vessel) of clear wine, and boil them together. When the gum ammoniac comes to a boil, all the others have boiled enough. If this remedy does not help, he should take a quarter of a *log* of milk of white goats, let it drip on three stalks of cabbage, and stir it with a stem of marjoram. When that stem comes to a boil, all the others have boiled enough. If even this remedy does not help, he should take the excrement of a white dog and knead it with balsam. If he can possibly avoid it, he should not resort to eating the dog's excrement, as it disintegrates the limbs (*Gittin* 69a–b).

16. Remedy for Swelling of the Spleen: For swelling of the spleen, a man should take seven water leeches and dry them in the shade, and every day drink two or three in wine. If this does not help, he should take the spleen of a she-goat that has not yet had young, put it inside an oven, stand by it, and say, "As this spleen has dried up, so may the spleen of so-and-so, son of so-and-so dry up." If this remedy does not help, he should look for the corpse of a person who died on the Sabbath, take the corpse's hand, put it against his own spleen, and say, "As the hand of this one has dried up, so may the spleen of so-and-so, son of so-and-so dry up" (*Gittin* 69b).

17. How to Restore Virility: Abaye said: "One who is unsure of his virility should bring three small measures of thorny saffron, pound it, boil it in wine, and drink it." Rabbi Yochanan said, "This is exactly what restored me to the vigor of my youth" (*Gittin* 70a).

18. How to Restore Strength to the Heart: Abaye said: "My mother told me that one who suffers from weakness of the heart should get meat from the right leg of a ram and dried cattle excrement dropped during the month of Nisan. If one has no dried cattle droppings, one should get chips of willow and roast the meat over them. One should then eat it and then drink diluted wine" (*Eruvin* 29b).

19. Remedy for a Scorpion Bite: Abaye said: "My mother told me that a six-year-old child stung by a scorpion on his birthday is not likely to live. What is a remedy? The gall of a white stork in beer. This is to be rubbed into the wound, and the rest should be given to the child to drink. A one-year-old stung by a wasp on his birthday is also not likely to live. What is a remedy? The bast of a date palm in water. This should be rubbed into the wound, and the rest should be given to the child to drink" (*Ketubot* 50a).

20. Remedy for a Wound to the Body: Samuel said: "A wound is to be regarded as so dangerous that the Sabbath may be profaned for it. What is the remedy? To stop the bleeding, pepperwort in vinegar; to induce new growth of flesh, peelings of cynodon and the paring of a thornbush, or worms from a dunghill" (*Avodah Zarah* 28a).

21. Remedy for a Growth on the Eye: Rabbi Safra said: "A berry-sized growth on the eye is an emissary of the angel of death. What is the remedy? Rue in honey or parsley in an inferior wine. In the meantime, a berry resembling it in size should be brought and rolled over it. A white berry for a white growth, and a black berry for a black growth" (*Avodah Zarah* 28a).

22. Remedy for a Bacterial Infection: Rava said: "A bacterial infection is a forerunner of a fever. What is the remedy? It should be snapped sixty times with the middle finger and then cut open crosswise and lengthwise. This should be done only if its head is not white. If its head is white, it is not dangerous" (*Avodah Zarah* 28a).

23. Remedy for a Fissure in the Rectum: When Rabbi Jacob was suffering from a fissure in the rectum, Rabbi Ammi (some say Rabbi Assi) directed him to take seven grains from the purple alkali plant, wrap them in a shirt collar, tie around it a white wool thread, dip the poultice in white naphtha, burn it, and powder the fissure with the ashes. While preparing the poultice, he was to take kernels of the nut of a thornbush and apply their split to the fissure. This should be done if the fissure is external. What should be done if it is internal? One should take some fat of a she-goat that has borne no young, melt it, and apply it inside the anus. If this remedy does not help, one should take three melon leaves that have been dried in the shade, burn them, and powder the fissure with the ashes. If this remedy does not help, one should apply olive oil mixed with wax and cover the fissure with strips of linen in summer and cotton wool in winter (*Avodah Zarah* 28a–28b).

24. Remedy for an Earache: Rabbi Abahu had an earache. So Rabbi Yochanan (some say the sages in the house of study) instructed him to take the kidney of a hairless goat, cut it crosswise and lengthwise, put it over glowing coals, and pour the water that comes out of it—neither hot nor cold, but tepid—into the ear. If this remedy did not work, he should take the fat of a large scarab beetle, melt it, and let it drip into the ear. If this remedy did not work, the ear should be filled with oil. Then seven wicks should be made out of clover stocks, with a garlic stem and a woolen tassel attached to one end of each wick, and the wick set alight. The other end should be placed inside the ear. The ear should be exposed to the fire, but care must be taken that there is no wind. Each wick should be replaced by another when it is used up. If this remedy did not work, he should take tow of the danda plant that has not been combed and place it within the ear, and place the ear near the fire. Care should be taken that there is no wind. If this remedy did not work, he should take the hundred-year-old tube of an old can, fill it with rock salt, then burn it and apply the ashes to the sore part of the ear (*Avodah Zarah* 28b).

25. Remedy for Scurvy: When Rabbi Yochanan suffered from scurvy, he went to a Roman noblewoman who prepared something for him on Thursday and Friday. What did she prepare for him? Rabbi Acha, son of Rabbi Ammi, said: "The water of leaven, olive oil, salt." Rabbi Yemar said: "Leaven itself, olive oil, and salt." Rabbi Ashi said: "The fat of a goose together with its wing." Abaye said: "I tried all of these without effecting a cure for myself, until an Arab recommended: 'Take the pits of olives that have not grown to one-third of their size, burn them in fire on a new rake, and stick them to the inside of the gums.' I did so and was cured" (*Yoma* 84a).

26. Remedy for Jaundice: "One afflicted by jaundice should be fed the flesh of a donkey. One bitten by a mad dog should be fed the lobe of its liver." So said Rabbi Matia ben Heresh. But the sages said: "There is no healing whatever in such remedies" (*Yoma* 84a).

27. Remedy for Worms in the Bowels: As a remedy for worms in the bowels, pennyroyal should be eaten. With what should it be eaten? With seven black dates. What causes worms in the bowels? Raw meat and water on an empty stomach, fat meat on an empty stomach, ox meat on an empty stomach, nuts on an empty stomach, or shoots of fenugreek eaten on an empty stomach and washed down with water. If there are no black dates, one should swallow with white cress. If that does not help, he should fast, then fetch some fat meat, put it over glowing coals, suck out the marrow from a bone, and gulp down vinegar. Not vinegar, others say, because it affects the liver. If that does not help, he should obtain the scrapings of a thornbush that was scraped from top to bottom—not from the bottom to the top, lest the worms issue through his mouth—and boil the scrapings in beer at twilight. The next day, he should hold his nose and make himself drink it. When he relieves himself, he should do so on the stripped parts of a date palm (*Shabbat* 109b).

28. Remedy for Drinking Uncovered Water: As an antidote for drinking uncovered water, one should drink juice of the shepherd's-flute plant. If that does not work, one should get five roses and five cups of beer, boil them together until the brew reduces to an *anpak* (a unit of liquid measure), and drink it. The mother of Rabbi Ahadboi bar Amni prepared a potion of one rose and one cup of beer for a certain man. She brought the mix to a boil and made him drink it. Then she lit the oven, swept it out to cool it, placed a brick on it, and had him sit on it to perspire, and the poison of the snake's venom oozed out of him in a liquid that was the color of a green leaf palm. Rabbi Ivia suggested as a remedy for uncovered water the following: a fourth of a *log* (a unit of liquid measure) of milk from a white goat. Rabbi Huna bar Judah said: "He should obtain a sweet *etrog* (citron), scoop it out, fill it with honey, set it over burning embers to boil, and then eat it." Rabbi Chanina said: "One should drink some urine forty days old as a remedy: A *barazina* (a unit of liquid measure) of it for a wasp sting; a fourth of a *log* for a scorpion's sting; and a half of a *log* for uncovered water. A *log* of urine is effective even against witchcraft (*Shabbat* 109b).

29. Remedy for Swallowing a Baby Snake: One who swallows a baby snake should eat cuscuta with salt and run three *mil*. Rabbi Shimi bar Ashi saw a man swallow a baby snake. He appeared to the man in the guise of a horseman and made him eat cuscuta with salt and run three *mil* before him, and the snake issued from the man rib by rib.

He who is bitten by a snake should obtain the embryo of a white she-ass, tear it open, and put it over him, provided however that the ass was not found to be suffering from a serious organic disease.

A certain officer of Pumbedita was once bitten by a snake. Now, there were thirteen white she-asses in Pumbedita. All were torn open, and each was found to be suffering from a serious organic disease. There was another she-ass on the outskirts of the city, but before they could go and bring it, a lion devoured it. Then Abaye suggested, "Perhaps this officer was bitten by the snake of the sages, for which there is no cure." The people replied, "This is so, our master, for when Rav died, Rabbi Isaac bar Bisna decreed that in token of mourning, myrtles and palm branches should not be brought to a wedding feast to the sound of bells, yet this officer did go and bring myrtles and palm branches to a wedding feast to the sound of bells." So a snake bit him, and he died.

If a snake winds itself around a person, that one should wade into water, put a basket over his head, and dislodge the snake. When the snake climbs up to the basket, he should shove the basket onto the water, go up out of the water, and get away quickly.

When a man is scented by a snake, if he has a companion with him, he should ride upon the companion's shoulders a distance of four cubits. If he has no companion, he should jump over a ditch full of water. If there is no ditch, he should ford a river. At night he should place his bed on four casks and sleep out-of-doors under the vault of heaven. He should also bring four she-cats and tie them to the four legs of the bed, then scatter chips of wood all around, so that when the cats hear the sound of the snake coming over the chips, they will devour it.

He who is chased by a snake should run toward sandy places (*Shabbat* 108b–110a).

30. Remedy for a Meat Bone Stuck in the Throat: He who has a meat bone stuck in his throat should bring more of that kind of meat, place it on his head, and say, "One by one, go down, swallow; swallow, go down, one by one." If it is a fish bone, he should say, "You are stuck like a pin, locked up as in a cuirass. Go down, go down" (*Shabbat* 67a).

31. Remedy for Bad Breath: It was said in the name of Rabbi Chiyya: After every food eat salt and after every beverage drink water and you will come to no harm. [One who does not do this] by day, he is liable to be troubled with an evil-smelling mouth (*Berachot* 40a).

32. Remedy for Foot Trouble: They were like a person who suffered with his feet and went around to all the doctors and could not find a cure until at last one came and said to him, "If you want to be cured, there is a very easy way of doing it: Plaster your feet with excrement of cattle" (Song of Songs Rabbah II, 3, 2).

33. Remedy for Heartburn: Rabbi Chama ben Chanina said: "One who takes black cumin regularly will not suffer heartburn (*Berachot* 40a).

CARING FOR THE BODY

The body is the soul's house (Philo Judaeus).

Human beings are created in the image of God, thus possessing dignity and value. Rabbinic authorities have always viewed the body as being imbued with sanctity. It is a gift from God, Who lends it to us for the duration of our lives, and we return it only upon our death.

Because of the underlying rabbinic principle that our bodies belong to God, many responsibilities related to the body emerge. First, we must take reasonable care of our bodies. Such obligations include proper hygiene (including bathing and wearing clean clothes), sleep, exercise, and proper diet.

A Talmudic Story on Body Care

Here is a story from the Talmud that illustrates one's responsibility to care for one's body.

The story is told of Hillel that when he had finished a lesson with his pupils, he accompanied them part

of the way. They said to him, "Master, where are you
going?" He answered, "To perform a religious duty."
They asked, "Which religious duty?" He responded,
"To bathe in the bath house." They questioned, "Is
this a religious obligation?" He replied, "If some-
body is appointed to scrape and clean the statues
of the king that are set up in the theaters and
circuses, and is paid to do the work, and furthermore associates with the nobility, how much more
so should I, who am created in the divine image
and likeness, take care of my body" (Leviticus
Rabbah 34:3).

In this conversation, Hillel makes the point that
not only must a person be concerned about his
knowledge and intellect, but he must also be concerned about the religious obligation of caring for
one's body. Thus Jews have an obligation to respect
and honor the body and to always treat it as one of
God's creations. During the time the body is in our
control, we may—and ought to—enjoy it, as long as
we use it in a manner that moves us and our body
toward holiness. Neglecting the body or abusing it
is a transgression that profanes the very name of
God.

In addition, we are obligated to avoid endanger-
ing our health. That is why Jewish law, for example, forbids a sick person from fasting on the
Day of Atonement, Yom Kippur. Such a fast might
cause further injury to a sick person. In addition, it
is the duty of a physician to heal the sick, and it is
the duty of human beings to seek out professional
medical attention when needed.

The Jewish mode for attaining holiness is to use all of one's bodily energies to perform God's commandments. Even bodily pleasures are positively commanded, including eating three festive meals in celebration of the holy Sabbath, bathing and wearing festive clothing in honor of the day, and enjoying the pleasures that come with lovemaking and propagation.

Bodily pleasures are best enjoyed when they have the specific goal of enhancing one's ability to do God's will and, thus, helping one to live a life of holiness. In the words of Maimonides:

> One who regulates one's life in accordance with the laws of medicine with the sole motive of maintaining a sound and vigorous physique and begetting children to do his work and labor for his benefit is not following the right course. A person should aim to maintain physical health and vigor in order that his soul may be upright, in a condition to know God. . . . Whoever throughout his life follows this course will be continually serving God, even while engaged in business and even during cohabitation, because his purpose in all that he does will be to satisfy his needs so as to have a sound body with which to serve God. Even when he sleeps and seeks repose to calm his mind and rest his body so as not to fall sick and be incapacitated from serving God, his sleep is service of the Almighty (Maimonides, *Mishneh Torah*, Laws of Ethics 3, 3).

Rabbi Yose the Galilean's Story: Everything in God's World Has a Counterpart in One's Body

In a most interesting passage quoted in the name of Rabbi Yose the Galilean, we are told that whatever God created in the world He also created in humans. Thus we see that the human body and all of its parts unite all that is above and all that is below. Here is this intriguing passage:

He created forests in the world and He created
  forests in man; to wit, man's hair;
He created evil beasts in the world and He created
  evil beasts in man: to wit, the vermin in man.
He created channels in the world and He created
  channels in man: to wit, man's ears.
He created a wind in the world and He created
  a wind in man: to wit, man's breath.
A sun in the world and a sun in man; to wit,
  man's forehead.
Stagnant waters in the world and stagnant waters
  in man: to wit, man's rheum.
Salt water in the world and salt water in man:
  to wit, man's tears.
Streams in the world and streams in man: to wit,
  man's urine.
Walls in the world and walls in man: to wit,
  man's lips.
Doors in the world and doors in man: to wit,
  man's teeth.
Firmaments in the world and firmaments in man:
  to wit, man's tongue.

Sweet waters in the world and sweet waters in man:
  to wit, man's spittle.
Stars in the world and stars in man: to wit,
  man's cheeks;
Towers in the world and towers in man: to wit,
  man's neck.
Masts in the world and masts in man: to wit,
  man's arms.
Pegs in the world and pegs in man: to wit,
  man's fingers.
Kings in the world and kings in man: to wit,
  man's heart.
Clusters in the world and clusters in man: to wit,
  man's breasts.
Counselors in the world and counselors in man:
  to wit, man's reins.
Millstones in the world and millstones in man:
  to wit, man's stomach.
Mashing mills in the world and mashing mills in man:
  to wit, man's spleen.
Pits in the world and pits in man: to wit, man's navel.
Flowing waters in the world and flowing waters
  in man: to wit, man's blood.
Trees in the world and trees in man: to wit,
  man's bones.
Hills in the world and hills in man: to wit,
  man's buttocks.
Pestle and mortar in the world and pestle and mortar
  in man: to wit, man's joints.
Horses in the world and horses in man: to wit,
  man's legs.
The angel of death in the world and the angel
  of death in man: to wit, man's heels.
Mountains and valleys in the world and mountains
  and valleys in man: erect, he is like a mountain;
  recumbent, he is like a valley.

Thus do you learn that whatever the Holy Blessed
One created in His world, He created in man
(*Avot de Rabbi Natan*, Chap. 31).

Book of the Pious:
The Correlation Between the Body and Foretelling the Future

In a fascinating passage that appears in the *Book of the Pious*, there is a correlation between one's body and foretelling the future:

> At the outset, let me say that God inscribed in the limbs of a man's body all that will transpire during his lifetime. And through the vibrations and twitches of a man's limbs, the Creator foretells what will happen to him each day. The source for this idea is the verse, "He takes account of my every step" [Job 31:4]. This teaches that the number of steps a man will take during his lifetime is predetermined; it is decreed how many steps he will walk. You can prove it to yourself. If the sole of your foot itches as if from a flea bite and after you scratch it the itch subsides, this is a sign that you will go on a trip to a place where you have never been before. If your ear itches, you can expect to hear a piece of news. If your eyelid tingles, you are going to see something new or receive tidings in a letter. If your tongue tickles, you will have news to report. If you feel your eyebrows itch, you are going to meet people you have not seen in a long time. If you have a sensation on your forehead, people are eagerly looking forward to seeing you; if on your hands, you will come into money; if on your nose, you will

become angry; if on your cheek, you will have cause
for weeping. And so it is with every limb in your
body; an itch is a harbinger of something new that
will happen in connection with this limb.

Who makes these portents happen? It is the Holy
One, blessed be He, telling you through your limbs
what is about to happen to you. Man should realize
that God preordains everything: how many steps he
is going to take, how many people he is going to
meet, how many things he is going to see, how many
things he is going to do, and how many words he is
going to speak. And so it is with each and every
limb. He should use the predetermined actions in
the pursuit of the moral life rather than to commit
transgressions . . . (*Sefer Chasidim*).

The *Code of Jewish Law* best sums up the rabbinic
attitude toward caring for the body in these two
passages.

Since it is the will of the Almighty that man's body
be kept healthy and strong, because it is impossible for a man to have any knowledge of his
Creator when ill, it is therefore his duty to shun
anything that may waste his body, and to strive to
acquire habits that will help him to become healthy.
Thus it is written [Deuteronomy 4:15]: "Take you,
therefore, good heed of your souls" (*Code of Jewish
Law*, condensed version, chap. 32).

Our rabbis, of blessed memory, said (*Berachot* 63a):
"Which is a short verse upon which all the principles of the Torah depend? It is Proverbs 3:6: 'In
all ways we must acknowledge God.' This means

that in all of our actions, even those we do in order
to sustain life, we must acknowledge God, and do
them for the sake of God's name, Blessed be the
One. For instance, eating, drinking, walking, sitting, lying down, rising, having sexual intercourse,
talking—all acts performed to sustain life should
be done for the sake of worshipping our Creator, or
doing something that will be conducive to the service of God" (*Code of Jewish Law*, condensed version, Chap. 31).

NOTABLE QUOTATIONS RELATED TO CARE OF THE BODY

The following quotations related to care of the
body derive from various rabbinic and midrashic
sources. Each reference sheds light on different
aspects of body care.

1. The Danger of Long Steps: Long steps take
away one-five-hundredth of a person's sight (*Berachot* 43b).

2. Where to Lie: Ben Azzai said: "Lie on anything,
but not on the ground" (*Berachot* 43b).

3. Diminishing a Person's Strength: Three things
sap a person's strength: worry, travel, and sin (*Gittin* 70a).

4. The Sigh: Rav said: "A sigh breaks half a man's
body" (*Berachot* 58b).

5. The Importance of Sleep: Samuel said: "Sleep at the break of dawn is as important as tempering is for iron" (*Berachot* 62b).

6. Hourly Advice: Our rabbis taught: "The first hour of the day is the time for the principal meal for gladiators; the second hour, for brigands; the third, for heirs; the fourth, for the generality; the fifth, for workmen; the sixth, for students of the wise. After that, it is like throwing a stone into a bottle" (*Shabbat* 10a).

7. The Importance of Vegetables: It is forbidden to live in a city that does not have a vegetable garden (Jerusalem Talmud *Kiddushin* 4:12, 66d).

8. Strong Bones: God will make your bones strong [Isaiah 58:11]. Rabbi Eleazar said: "This is the most perfect of blessings" (*Yevamot* 102b).

9. Rava's Advice: Rav said to his son Chiyya: "Don't fall into the habit of taking drugs, don't leap over a sewer, don't have your teeth pulled, and don't provoke serpents" (*Pesachim* 113a).

10. The Healing Power of the Sun: "The saving sun with healing in its wings" [Malachi 3:20]. Abaye said: "This proves that the shining sun brings healing (*Nedarim* 8b).

HYGIENE

The main contribution of talmudic medicine lies not so much in the treatment of illness, but rather, as in the Bible, in the prevention of disease and the care of community health. The hygienic methods advocated were of a practical nature as well as of a religious, ethical nature. A principle that recurs a number of times is that "Bodily cleanliness leads to spiritual cleanliness" (*Avodah Zarah* 20b, Jerusalem Talmud *Shabbat* 1:3, 3b). Hygienic regulations applied to town planning, climatic conditions, social community life, family life, and care of the body. The following is a cross-section of references related to the topic of hygiene culled from rabbinic sources.

1. Washing the Hands: The first thing to do upon arising in the morning is to wash one's hands, because of the germs that have gathered there during one's sleep (Testament of Rabbi Eliezer the Great).

2. Beneficial Germs: No matter what a person touches, he gets germs on his hands, but there are also beneficial bacteria that combat their effect (*Shochar Tov* 17, *Yalkut Shimoni*, Psalms 42:6).

3. Breath and Germs: The breath of a sick person contains germs from his sickness (Rabbi Eliezer the Great).

4. The Benefits of Perspiration: Perspiration that is the result of sickness, bathing, or work is beneficial to the body (*Avot de Rabbi Natan*, 41).

5. Advice on Clothing: Clothes worn during the day should not be worn at night (*Menachot* 43).

6. Advice on Housing and Spaciousness: A house that is not sufficiently spacious is not fit to be called a dwelling (*Sukkah* 3).

7. Window Advice: Windows should be constructed wide on the interior and narrow on the exterior so as to draw in the air (Leviticus Rabbah 31).

8. On Bathrooms: Every house should have a bathroom and toilet as well as a dining room (*Berachot* 8, *Baba Metzia* 107, *Shabbat* 25).

9. Hand-Washing After Using the Lavatory: Hands should always be washed before leaving the toilet (*Pirkei Rabbeninu HaKodesh*).

10. Advice About Coins in One's Mouth: Coins should not be placed in the mouth because they may have been touched by persons suffering from contagious diseases (Maimonides, *Mishneh Torah*, Rotzeach 12, 4).

11. Rinsing Cups: Rinse your cup before and after drinking from it (*Tamid* 27b).

12. Washing the Hands Before Eating: Those who eat food with unwashed hands endanger their health, because they are full of dangerous germs (*Yoma* 77b).

13. Washing Body Parts: The face, hands, and feet should be washed every day (*Shabbat* 50b).

14. Dealing with Infected Clothing: Mention is made of seven ingredients used for cleansing infected clothing (*Zevachim* 95a).

15. Advice on Where Not to Dig a Well: Digging of wells in the neighborhood of cemeteries or garbage dumps is forbidden (*Baba Batra* 1:10).

DIET

It is a well-known medical fact that proper eating habits and diet have a major effect on one's health, both body and mind. Overeating and being overweight can cause shortness of breath and heart problems. Some biblical commentators have read into biblical passages the idea of vegetarianism as a way of life. In the Creation narrative (Genesis 29:30), for instance, both humans and the animals are given the herbs of the field for their food, and they are not to prey on each other. Adam and Eve, the ideal man and woman, inhabitants of the Garden of Eden, eat only fruits and vegetables. No mention is made of animals as Adam's food, only "herb-yielding seed" and "every tree in which is the fruit of a tree-yielding seed." Not until we come to the story of Noah does the Bible indicate permission for the human consumption of meat. Interestingly, some of today's medical research seems to indicate that eating too much red meat is not good for one's health. The following are some rabbinic quotations, sayings, and advice related to diet.

1. The Deleterious Effects of Fasting: Fasting weakens the body and blackens the teeth (Lamentations Rabbah 1, *Chagiga* 22).

2. Eating Improper Food: One who denies himself proper food is considered a sinner (*Taanit* 11).

3. Appetizing Food: Food should be appetizing as well as nourishing (*Yoma* 74).

4. Talking While Eating: Talking while eating may cause choking, as may eating while lying on one's back or reclining to one's right (*Pesachim* 108).

5. The Importance of Cutting One's Food: Cutting one's food and eating it is better than biting off pieces and swallowing them (*Berachot* 74).

6. Overeating: Overeating causes sickness (*Ben Sira* 37).

7. Tempting Food: Food that is tempting is easily digested (*Sefer Raziel HaMalach* 13).

8. Soup and the Meal: A meal without soup is no meal (*Bereachot* 44).

9. When to Eat Solid Foods: Up to the age of forty, solid foods are better than liquids (*Shabbat* 152).

10. When to Eat Sweets: Sweets are best after a meal (Ruth Rabbah 3, 7).

11. Dessert Foods: Dates, roasted grains, and nuts are good for dessert (*Pesachim* 119).

12. Advice to Prevent Intestinal Trouble: A properly balanced diet, avoidance of overeating, and attention to the calls of nature on time prevent intestinal trouble (*Gittin* 70).

13. The Dangers of Overeating: More people die from overeating than from hunger (*Shabbat* 33a).

14. Advice on How Much to Eat: Eat a third of your capacity, drink a third, and leave the remaining third empty. Then, if you become angry, there is room for the stomach to expand (*Gittin* 70a).

15. Advice on Eating Meat: One should not eat meat twice in one day (*Yoma* 75).

16. The Importance of Chewing Food: Chewing food is essential to health (*Niddah* 65a).

17. Eating Meat: One should not eat meat unless one has a special appetite for it (*Chullin* 84a).

18. Bread, Salt, and Water: Bread with salt in the morning and plenty of water will banish all illnesses (*Baba Kamma* 92b).

19. Meal Regulation: Meal regulation is important to one's health; eat when hungry and drink when thirsty (*Berachot* 62b).

20. Eating While Standing: Eating or drinking while standing shatters a person's body (*Gittin* 70a).

21. Eating and Traveling: When traveling, one should eat sparingly, as otherwise disorder of the bowels may result (*Taanit* 10b).

22. Advice About Cheese: Cheese that is one day old is the most healthful (*Shabbat* 134).

23. Milk and the Teeth: The properties of milk whiten the teeth (Midrash Bereshit 49, 12).

24. The Therapeutic Value of Sweet Apples: Sweet apples are a remedy for almost every ailment (*Zohar* 3, 74).

25. Advice For Drinking Wine: Wine drunk during a meal will not intoxicate, but wine drunk after a meal will (Jerusalem Talmud, *Pesachim* 10, 6).

26. The Importance of Breakfast: Breakfast is the most important meal of the day, as it has thirteen advantages. It protects from heat, cold, wind, evil spirits; brightens the intellect of the fool; helps one win a lawsuit; helps one learn; helps one teach; makes one's words listened to and retained by one's listeners; keeps one's flesh from emitting excessive heat; makes one have affection for one's wife and not lust after a strange woman; kills intestinal parasites. To these, some add, it removes jealousy and substitutes love (*Baba Batra* 107b).

27. Laxative Foods and Binding Foods: Foods of laxative effect—such as grapes, figs, mulberries, pears, melons, certain species of cucumbers, and melopepons should be eaten at the beginning of a meal, and one should wait a bit before eating the regular food thereafter. Foods that are binding, such as pomegranates, quinces, and apples, should be eaten at the conclusion of the meal.

If the menu contains both fowl and beef, the fowl should be eaten first. If eggs and fowl, the eggs should be eaten first. Lean and fat meat, the lean meat first—the general rule being that the lighter food should always precede the heavier.

In the summer, cool foods should be eaten, and the use of spices should be avoided. In the winter, warm foods should be eaten, and they may be liberally spiced if desired.

Certain foods are particularly injurious to the system, such as large, salted, old fish; stale, salted cheese; certain species of mushrooms; aged, salted meat; unfermented wine; foods that have become stale and odoriferous; and all foods that have a vile odor or are particularly bitter. They are all like poison to the body.

There are other foods that, while not dangerous, are not especially wholesome, and these should be eaten only in moderation and infrequently, such as large fish, old cheese, milk more than twenty-four hours old, flesh of a large bull or he-goat, beans, lentils, peas, barley bread, mustard, radish, unleavened bread, cabbage, leek, and onions. These should be eaten sparingly, and only in the winter. Pumpkins and similar gourds should be eaten only in the summer.

Figs, grapes, and nuts are exceptionally wholesome, either fresh or dried. Unripe fruits are like a sword piercing the body. Honey and wine are bad for youngsters, but excellent for the aged, particularly in wintertime. During the summer, a normal diet should be about two-thirds of what is eaten during the winter.

The individual who is wise controls his appetite, and refrains from eating any food that is harmful unless it is required for curative purposes.

Regular, punctual, elimination is desirable and essential for well-being. Constipation is a warning of approaching serious ailments. As long as a man works hard, does not eat to his full capacity, as long as his eliminative organs function smoothly and properly, no ailment will visit him, and his strength will remain and increase. But he who sits idle, takes no exercise, and is constipated, although he may eat good food and take medicinal precautions, will suffer pain all his life and his strength will fade. Gluttony is as deadly as poison, and is the basis of most illness. For most diseases are caused by either improper food or eating to excess (Maimonides, *Mishneh Torah*, Hilchot De'ot, 4, 6–15).

28. The Properties of Garlic: Five things were said of garlic: It satisfies hunger, keeps the body warm, makes the face bright, increases a person's potency, and kills parasites in the bowels (*Baba Kamma* 82a).

29. Eating Disagreeable Food: One who eats foods that do not agree with him transgresses three commandments, in that he has despised himself, despised the foods, and recited a blessing improperly (*Avot de Rabbi Natan*, Chap. 6).

30. Eating Moderately: The moderate eater enjoys healthy sleep. He rises early, feeling refreshed. But sleeplessness, indigestion, and colic are the lot of the glutton (*Code of Jewish Law*, condensed version, Chap. 32).

31. Advice on When to Eat And Drink: One should eat only when justified by a feeling of hunger, the stomach is clear, and the mouth possesses saliva. Then one is really hungry. A person must not drink water unless truly justified by thirst. This means that if one feels hungry or thirsty one should wait a while, as occasionally one is led to feel so by a deceptive hunger and deceptive thirst (*Code of Jewish Law*, condensed version, Chap. 32).

32. Adam and Noah and Permission to Eat Meat: Adam was not permitted to eat meat, for it is written: "See, I give you every seed-bearing plant that is upon the Earth. And to all the animals on land, to all the birds in the sky, and to everything that creeps on earth, I give all the green plants for food" [Genesis 1:29, 30]. The implication is that the beasts of the Earth shall not be for man to eat.

But at the time of the sons of Noah, meat was permitted, for it is said: "Every creature that live shall be yours to eat . . . [Genesis 9:3] (*Sanhedrin* 59b).

33. Wine and Its Benefits: The benefits of wine are many if it is taken in the proper amount, as it keeps the body in a healthy condition and cures many illnesses. But the knowledge of its consumption is hidden from the masses. What they want is to get drunk, and inebriety causes harm (Maimonides, *Preservation of Youth*).

EXERCISE

Exercise is recognized today as having real health benefits. The rabbinic sages also realized the therapeutic benefits of regular exercise. Following are some passages showing what various Jewish sources have to say about exercise and its health benefits.

1. One does not consider exercise, though it is the main principle in keeping one's health and in

the repulsion of most illnesses. . . . And there is no such thing as excessive body movements and exercise. Because body movements and exercise will ignite natural heat and superfluities will be formed in the body, they will be expelled. However, when the body is at rest, the natural heat is suppressed and the superfluities remain. . . . Exercise removes the harm caused by most bad habits, which most people have. And no movement is as beneficial, according to the physicians, as body movements and exercise. Exercise refers to both strong and weak movements, provided it is movement that is vigorous and affects breathing, increasing it. Violent exercise causes fatigue, and not everyone can stand fatigue, or needs it. It is good for the preservation of health to shorten the exercises (Maimonides, *The Preservation of Youth*).

2. Anyone who sits around idle and takes no exercise will be subject to physical discomforts and failing strength, even though one eats wholesome food and takes care of oneself in accordance with medical advice (*Code of Jewish Law*, condensed version, Chap. 31).

3. Strenuous exercise should be taken every day in the morning until the body begins to get warm. Then one should rest a little until one is refreshed, and eat. If one takes a warm bath after exercise, so much the better (Maimonides, *Mishneh Torah*, Hilchot Yesodei HaTorah, Hilchot De'ot, Chap. 4).

4. It is a known rule in medical science that before eating a person should have some exercise,

by walking or by working until one's body becomes warm, and thereafter eat. And concerning this it is written [Genesis 3:1]: "With the sweat of your face you shall eat bread." And again [Proverbs 31:27]: "And the bread of idleness she does not eat" (*Code of Jewish Law*, condensed version, Chap. 32).

HEALING IN
JEWISH LITURGY

Our Father, our King, send complete healing to the sick (*Avinu Malkenu*).

In both biblical and rabbinic times, prayers were used in time of illness. The Patriarch Abraham prayed for the recovery of Avimelech (Genesis 20:17), and God healed him. David prayed for the recovery of his son (2 Samuel 12:16), but his son died. Elisha prayed for the recovery of the Shunammite woman's son (2 Kings 4:33), and the boy recovered. King Hezekiah prayed for his own recovery (2 Chronicles 32:24), and God added an additional fifteen years to his life. The shortest prayer on record is the famous prayer uttered by Moses for the recovery of his sister, Miriam, who was afflicted with leprosy. Moses said: *El na refa na la* (O God, heal her, I beseech You), and she recovered (Numbers 12:13).

Many prayers are found in the *siddur* that relate to both the care of one's body and the image of God as Healer. Following are some examples of such prayers.

115

1. *Modeh Ani* **(I Am Grateful to You):** *Modeh Ani* is a prayer that is based on the interpretation of the verse "They are new every morning; great is Your faithfulness" (Lamentations 3:23). It is customarily recited immediately upon awakening in the morning. With this prayer, we daily thank God for renewing our physical and mental abilities. We also praise God's dependability in maintaining a regular and orderly cycle of nature. Here are the words of the prayer:

> I am grateful to you, living and enduring King, for restoring my soul to me in compassion. You are faithful beyond measure.

2. *Adon Olam* **(Lord Eternal):** This prayer is one of the most popular hymns added to Jewish liturgy since biblical times. Its author is conjectured to be Solomon ibn Gabirol of Spain, the renowned eleventh-century poet. The concluding verses of the prayer aver that we need not be afraid when we go to sleep, because God will always be there to protect us. Here are the two concluding verses:

> He is my God, my life's redeemer, my refuge in distress, My shelter sure, my cup of life, His goodness is limitless. I place my spirit in His care, when I wake as when I sleep. God is with me, I shall not fear, body and spirit in His keep.

3. *Asher Yatzar* **(You Fashioned the Human Body):** This ancient prayer is one of the first ones recited in the morning and appears early in the prayerbook. It is traditionally said privately by each worshipper before the commencement of the worship service itself. Common practice is to recite it after having relieved oneself. It sometimes is used today after having one's physical exam and receiving the good news that one is in good health.

The prayer praises God for creating the wondrous mechanism of the body and for preserving our health and our lives. It reflects the importance that Judaism attaches to proper health care, and is also a reminder that our bodies belong to God and that we must do everything in our power to take proper care of our bodies. God, in this prayer, is referred to as Healer of all flesh.

Here is the prayer:

Praised are You, O Sovereign our God, Ruler of the Universe, Who with wisdom fashioned the human body, creating openings, arteries, glands, and organs, marvelous in structure, intricate in design. Should but one of them, by being blocked, fail to function, it would be impossible to exist. Praised are You, Lord, Healer of all flesh Who sustains our bodies in wondrous ways.

4. *Elohai Neshama* (My God, the Soul You Gave Me Is Pure): The theme of this ancient prayer is for the worshipper to show his gratefulness to God for the gift of the soul. The realization of the divine Source of one's soul is meant to strengthen a person to meet the tasks and temptations of daily life. The doctrine of the immortality of the soul is also affirmed in this prayer:

O my God, the soul you gave me is pure. You created and formed it, and you did breathe it into me. You preserved it within me, and you will take it from me, but will restore it to me in the hereafter. So long as the soul is within me, I will give thanks to you, O God and God of my ancestors, Sovereign of all works, Lord of all souls. Blessed are You, O Lord, who restores souls to the dead.

5. Psalm 147: Recited each day as part of the morning preliminary service, Psalm 147 (verse 3) has an important reference to God as Healer.

God heals the broken-hearted and binds up their wounds.

6. *Le El Baruch* (To Praiseworthy God): This prayer is recited before the Shema. It praises God for His uniqueness and His ability to perform mighty deeds, including that of bringing healing. Here are the opening lines of the prayer:

To praiseworthy God they [the angels] sweetly sing; the living, enduring God, they celebrate in song. For God is unique, doing mighty deeds, creating new life, championing justice, sowing righteousness, reaping victory, bringing healing. . . .

7. Amidah (The Standing Prayer): This ancient prayer, recited daily, consists of nineteen different blessings. These portions of the *Amidah* refer to the healing qualities of God:

He . . . supports the fallen, heals the sick, frees the fettered. Heal us, O Lord, and we shall be healed. Help us and save us for You are our glory. Grant perfect healing for all our afflictions. For You are the faithful and merciful God of healing. Praised are You, Lord, Who heals the sick of His people Israel.

8. *Avinu Malkenu* **(Our Father, Our King):** This prayer is recited between Rosh Hashanah and Yom Kippur, as well as on fasting days. It consists of a series of invocations and supplications to God, and has a reference to healing in its twelfth line:

Our Father, our King, send complete healing to those who are ill.

9. *Birkat Hagomel* **(Blessing of Thanksgiving):** Persons who have safely returned from some hazardous voyage, or have recovered from serious illness, are required to offer thanks to God in a benediction recited in addition to the Torah blessings when they are called to the public Torah reading in the synagogue. This benediction, known as *birkat hagomel,* is derived from Psalm 107, according to talmudic interpretation (*Berachot* 54b). Psalm 107 begins by calling upon the exiles, brought back to their homes, to give thanks. Then it describes God's goodness in taking care of lost travelers, prisoners, the sick, and sea voyagers. The refrain at the end of each of the four stanzas reads: "Let them thank God for His kindness and His wonders toward people."

When the *birkat hagomel* blessing is recited by an entire community, it is of a soul-stirring character. On Friday evening, December 14, 1940, the enemy bombing of a city in England resulted in 587 deaths, among them a number of Jews. The next morning, when the Jewish worshippers recited the *birkat hagomel* blessing in thanksgiving for their delivery, there was not a dry eye in the synagogue.

Birkat hagomel, which is customarily offered by a group of ten or more worshippers—ten being the minimum required for congregational worship— reads as follows:

Praised are You, O Sovereign our God, Ruler of the universe, who bestows favors on the undeserving and has shown me every kindness.

Upon hearing this blessing, the congregation responds:

May God who has shown you every kindness continue to favor you with all that is good.

10. *Mi Shebayrach* (May God Who Has Blessed): The well known Hebrew prayer for the community, which begins with the Hebrew words *mi shebayrah* (He who has blessed) is recited after the reading of the Torah. Included in the daily prayerbook are variations of this prayer for such occasions as naming a newborn daughter; on behalf of persons called to the Torah; and on behalf of those who are ill. Here is the wording of this prayer for one who is ill:

May God who blessed our ancestors Abraham, Isaac, and Jacob, Sarah, Rebecca, Rachel, and Leah, bless and heal————. May the Holy One in kindness strengthen him (her) and heal him (her) speedily, body and soul, together with all others who are ill. And let us say: Amen.

11. *Vidui* (Confessional): If it is perceived that the sick person is soon to die, a special prayer, in the form of a confession, is to be recited. Following is a brief form of this confession:

O God and God of my ancestors, let my prayer come before You, and do not disregard my supplication. O forgive all the sins which I have committed from my birth until this day. I am abashed and ashamed of my evil deeds and transgressions. Pray accept my pain and suffering as an expiation, and forgive my wrongdoing, for against You alone have I sinned.

May it be Your will, O Lord my God and God of my ancestors, that I sin no more, and purge the sins I have committed with full mercy, not by means of affliction and diseases. O send for me, and for all sick persons in Israel, a perfect cure and healing.

I acknowledge unto You, O Lord my God and God of my ancestors, that both my cure and my death depend upon Your will. May it be Your will to heal me. Yet if you have decreed that I shall die of this disease, may my death expiate all the sins, iniquities, and transgressions that I have committed before You. Grant me shelter in the shadow of Your wings and a portion in *Gan Eden*, and let me merit the resurrection and the life of bliss in the world-to-come, which is reserved for the righteous.

Father of the orphan and Judge of the widow, protect my beloved kindred, with whose souls my soul is bound up.

Into Your hand I commit my spirit; You have redeemed me, O God of truth.

Hear O Israel, the Lord our God, the Lord is One.
The Lord, He is God.

12. Prayer and the Order of Adding a Name: The
sages of the Talmud said (*Rosh Hashanah* 16b):
"Four things cause an evil decree passed upon a
person to be canceled. They are: charity, prayer,
adding a name, and change of action. Hence, the
custom prevails to add to the name of a sick person, in order to fool the angel of death. When the
sick person is blessed by adding on a new name,
the following prayer is recited:

Even if it were decreed against him (her) by Your
righteous Court that he (she) die of his (her) present
illness, lo, our holy rabbis said that three things
cause an evil decree passed on man to be canceled,
one of them being the change of the sick person's
name. We fulfilled what they said and his (her)
name was changed, and it is a different person. If
the decree was passed on——, but on——it was
not passed, for it is now someone else that is not
called by the former name. As his (her) name was
changed, so may the evil decree passed on him
(her) be changed from law to mercy, from death to
life, from illness to a perfect cure to——, son
(daughter) of——. In the name of the persons
mentioned in this Holy Book, and in the name of
Your angels that bring healing and relief, send
speedily a perfect cure to——, son (daughter)
of——, and prolong his (her) days and years with
health. May he (she) spend his (her) days in good
health and peace, from now and henceforth. Amen.
Selah.

TWENTIETH-CENTURY
HEALING PRAYERS

Many modern expressions of healing have been created by liturgists of all branches of Judaism. These prayers are used in Jewish healing services throughout the country. Following are some samples of modern-day healing expressions.

May the Source of strength Who helped the
   ones before us
Help us find the courage to make our lives
   a blessing.
And let us say: Amen.
Bless those in need of healing with *refuah shlayma,*
The renewal of body, the renewal of spirit
And let us say: Amen.

In sickness I turn to You, O God, for comfort and help. Strengthen within me the wondrous power of healing that You have implanted in Your children. Guide my doctors and nurses that they may speed my recovery. Let my dear ones find comfort and courage in the knowledge that You are with us at all times, in sickness and in health. May my sickness not weaken my faith in You, nor diminish my love for others. From my illness may I gain a fuller sympathy for all who suffer. I praise You, O God, the Source of healing (*CCAR Prayerbook*).

L'dor v'dor, God who has sustained us from
   generation to generation
Listen to my supplication
I pray to you on bended knee
Shine your countenance again upon me.

You cause the winds to blow, the rains to fall
Master of life and death, heal all.

There is healing for every pain
God grant me good health again.
Lord, who has made the Earth a generous mother,
To provide in plentiful abundance food for others.

Change the gloom of despair to the radiance
   of hope
Write my sins upon the sand and my virtue on
   the tablets
O merry heart doeth good like a medicine
Life is not merely being alive, but being well
   (Lou Feld).

A Patient's Prayer:

Eternal God, source of healing,
Out of distress I call upon You.
Help me to sense Your presence,
At this difficult time.
You have already sent me gifts of Your goodness:
The skill of my physician,
The concern of others who help me,
The compassion of those I love.
I pray that I may be worthy of all these,
Today and in the days to come.
Help me to banish all bitterness;
Let not despair overcome me.
Grant me patience when the hours are heavy;
Give me courage whenever there is hurt or
    disappointment.
Keep me trustful in Your love, O God.
Give me strength for today, and hope for tomorrow.
To Your loving hands I commit my spirit—
When asleep and when awake.
You are with me; I shall not fear.
Help me, O God, in my time of need.

Prayer Before an Operation:

O merciful Father, I turn to Thee in prayer.
Thou who bindest up wounds and healest the sick,
I put my trust in Thee.
Knowing that I am in Thy hands, O God,
I have faith that Thou wilt not forsake me.
Give me courage now and in the days ahead.
Grant wisdom and skill to my physician;
make all those who are assisting me
instruments of Thy healing power.
Give me strength for this day
and grant me hope for tomorrow.
Hear my prayer; be with me; protect me.
Restore me to health, O Lord,
so that I may serve Thee.
Heal me, O Lord, and I shall be healed;
Save me and I shall be saved;
For Thou art my praise (Jeremiah 17:14).
The Lord is with me, I shall not fear,
Hear, O Israel: The Lord Our God, the Lord is One.

A Prayer for Those Who Are Ill, and Their Care-
takers:

May the One who blesses all life, bless and heal
    these people who struggle against illness.
May those afflicted with disease be blessed with
    faith, courage, loving, and caring. May they
    know much support and sustenance from
    their friends, their loving companions,
    and their communities.
May they be granted a full and complete healing
    of body and soul.
May those who seek ways of healing through
    increased medical knowledge and those who
    care for the sick daily be blessed with
    courage, stamina, and communal support.
May all, the sick and the well together, be
    granted courage and hope. And let us say:
    Amen (Leila Gal Berner).

Early-Twentieth-Century Prayer for a Sick Husband:

From the depth of my heart I call upon Thee, O my Lord, awful is the darkness that surrounds me on account of the sickness of my beloved husband. With a contrite, anxious, and lacerated heart I implore Thee, that thou mayest preserve unto me, yet for many, many years, the precious treasure which Thou, in Thy grace, didst vouchsafe unto me.

Refreshed by no slumber or rest, the nights pass away before me; bitter woe is my severe companion, for the happiness of my family lies prostrate, the crown of my house is surrounded by dark clouds. O Lord! hearken unto my prayer, remove this heavy weight from my heart. Do not deprive me of the dearest and highest of all treasures, do not tear the heart from the heart!

But the hope written within my heart, by the belief of my fathers, speaks unto me with consoling words: "Confide, and endure, whatever the Lord may have ordained for thee!" Yes, I wait upon Thy paternal grace, I trust in Thy mercy, as the sacred bard teaches me: "He that trusteth in the Lord, mercy shall compass him about." Return, O God, unto my beloved husband his former strength and vigor, return him unto his sacred duties, and let him work, yet for many years, for the welfare of our family. Oh, may this be Thy holy will. Amen.

Early-Twentieth-Century Prayer for Sick Parents:

More in tears than in words is my prayer poured forth this day, before Thee, all-merciful Father, in tears burning and abundant, produced by woe and anxiety. For what is more saddening for the heart of a child than to know that a dear parent is prostrated upon the couch of sufferings and sickness? And however much I trust and hope in Thy mercy, yet with trembling and alarm I bow before Thee, to implore of Thee the life, the health of my beloved father (mother). Thou hast proclaimed the word: "Ye shall seek my face!" I seek Thy face with a longing heart. O do not hide it from me. Hearken unto my fervent prayer. Let not my tears flow in vain before Thee, have mercy upon my dear father (mother), quicken him (her) with the soft dew of Thy grace, mercifully pour Thy healing balm upon his (her) wounds, and let the rays of Thy goodness and compassion descend upon him (her), that he (she) may be uplifted by their warmth and restored to strength and vigor. Forgive him (her), O all-good Father! Whenever and wherever he (she) may have erred, and remember all the good and charitable deeds which he (she) may have performed. Let these deeds now intercede for him (her) before Thy throne of justice and mercy.

May my fervent prayer come before Thee, that the hour of deliverance and salvation may soon arrive, and our tears of woe be turned into tears of joy and gratitude. Amen.

Early-Twentieth-Century Prayer for a Sick Child:

O all-merciful Father, from the depth of my aggrieved heart I implore Thee: Spare my child, do not take away this treasure that Thou gavest unto me from Thine boundless grace and goodness. I know that this treasure is Thine, as all other boons which I call mine; Thou disposest of them, according to Thy holy will. O may it be Thy holy will to preserve for me this precious jewel. Once Thou spokest unto Thy suffering congregation: "Call unto me in need, and I shall hear thee!" And through the inspired Isaiah Thou gavest the consoling assurance unto Thy people Israel: "I will pour my spirit upon thy children, and my blessing upon thine offspring!" O extend this paternal promise also upon my child, grant him (her) health and long life.

And unto me grant strength in all the cares and trials of life, fortify my courage in the fulfillment of my duties and in the endurance of all the heavy burdens that Thy paternal hands may impose upon me. In Thee, O God, I trust, for Thou are nigh unto all who call upon Thee. Amen.

Early-Twentieth-Century Prayer in Heavy Sickness:

O Lord, answer and compassionate me, for I am full of distress, and humbled in mine afflictions. I am bowed down with weakness as a child, and without Thine aid, how shall I bear my troubles? O that my deeds had been worthy of Thine approbation, then had my soul been satisfied and my heart rejoiced. Yet, do Thou, O God, regard my contrition, hear my prayer, and lend Thy mercy even as a staff for my support. O Lord, pains and evils are inherited with the nature of man, yet my soul shall not be shaken by their approach. For on whom shall I call for help but on Thee? And where shall I rest my hope but in Thy mercies? "Though my flesh and my heart fail, God is my consolation, my portion forever; for lo, they that are far from Thee shall perish, they that go after the favor of others shall be destroyed." Ah! were my days of sorrow lengthened to the number of mine offenses, yet, O Lord, I would still bless Thy name, and Thy dispensations, for Thou art my consolation, the resting place of my soul. Then, wherefore should I complain? I will resign myself to Thy will, for Thou, O Lord are the Author of my being, and wilt not destroy the work which Thou has made. Then shall I profit from my woes, and all times rest in Thy hands; for Thou, O my God, art my Savior and my living Redeemer. Amen.

Twentieth-Century-Prayer on Recovery from Sickness:

O God, great, mighty, and revered, in the abundance of Thy lovingkindness I come before Thee to render thanks for all the benefits Thou hast bestowed upon me. In my distress I called upon Thee and Thou didst answer me; from my bed of pain I cried unto Thee and Thou didst hear the voice of my supplication. Thou hast chastened me sore, O Lord, but Thou didst not give me over unto death. In Thy love and pity Thou didst bring up my soul from the grave. For Thy anger is but for a moment; Thy favor is for a lifetime: Weeping may tarry for the night, but joy cometh in the morning. The living, the living, he shall praise Thee, as I do this day, and my soul that Thou didst redeem shall tell Thy wonders unto the children of men. Blessed are Thou, the faithful Physician unto all flesh.

O God, merciful and gracious, Who dispensest kindnesses to the undeserving, I am indeed unworthy of all the mercies Thou hast hitherto shown unto me. O purify my heart that I may be fit to walk in the way of the upright before Thee; and continue Thy help unto Thy servant. Restore me to perfect health, and with bodily vigor bless me. Remove from me all sorrow and care, preserve me from all evil, and guide me with Thine own counsel; so shall the sun of righteousness arise unto me with healing in its wings.

Let the words of my mouth and the meditation of my heart be acceptable before thee, O Lord, my Rock and my Redeemer. Amen.

HEALING PSALMS

Watch over me, God, for I seek refuge in You
(Psalms 16:1).

Recitation of daily psalms, at times of joy or
trouble, has been an accepted Jewish tradition for
generations. Tradition has ascribed the writing of
the book of Psalms to King David, and several of
the psalms appear to have been composed when
the king was bedridden with illness. The recital of
the whole book of Psalms is widespread, whether
as an act of piety by saintly individuals or by
groups of unlearned people. For this purpose,
"societies of reciters of psalms" were formed, and
in recent times a special society has been formed
in Jerusalem whereby two separate groups recite
the whole book of Psalms daily at the Western
Wall.

Throughout the ages, the Jewish people have
used various psalms for purposes of praying for the
sick, including praying for themselves when illness strikes. Many of these psalms have common
values and ideas. They include the following: God
is a Healer and has the power to heal the sick if the

sick person puts his or her trust in God; when praying for one's own recovery or for the recovery of another, one's intention should be to pray for health so that the sick should become well in order to serve God; God wants to do goodness, and God's kindness extends to everyone and everything.

Years ago, the eighteenth-century Hassidic master Rabbi Nachman of Breslov identified ten specific psalms as having particular power to bring a true and complete healing of both body and spirit. He designated these ten psalms (16, 32, 41, 42, 59, 77, 90, 105, 137, and 150) as the *Tikkun Haklali*—the Complete Remedy. Rabbi Nachman also recommended other ingredients that were necessary in order to enhance the efficaciousness of the psalm recital. These ingredients included giving to charity; immersing in a ritual bath (*mikveh*)—or, if this were impossible, to perform the ritual hand-washing ceremony before reciting the psalm; invoking the names of *tzaddikim* (righteous people) and, if possible, visiting their graves (the memory of such people was said to have healing powers).

Following are Rabbi Nachman's ten psalms of healing.

1. Psalm 16: In this psalm, commentators have stated that the psalmist is ill and asks for God's protection. The psalmist rejoices that God will not abandon his soul in this world or in the world-to-come.

Keep me, O God, for I have taken refuge in You.
I have said to God: "You are my God;

I have no good but in You";
As for the holy that are in the earth,
They are the excellent in whom is all of my delight.
Let the idols of them be multiplied
That make suit unto another.
Their drink-offerings of blood will I not offer
Nor take their names upon my lips.
O God, the portion of my inheritance and my cup
You maintain my lot.
The lines are fallen unto me in pleasant places
I have a good heritage.
I will bless God, who has given me counsel
Though at night my conscience afflicts me.
I have always set God before me.
Surely God is at my right hand, I shall not be
    moved.
Therefore, my heart is glad and my glory rejoices
My flesh also dwells in safety.
For You will not abandon my soul to the nether
    world
Neither will You let the one who loves You see
    his own grave.
You make known to me the path of life
In Your presence is fullness of joy.
In Your right hand is everlasting bliss.

2. Psalm 32: This psalm expresses the serious consequences, both physical and mental, that may follow from disharmony within the soul. Once the psalmist confesses his sin (perhaps King David's infidelity with Batsheba), God in His infinite love forgives the iniquity, feeling the pain and hurt of the psalmist. The psalm concludes with a note of exaltation and offers a reminder to all that God will save and heal those who trust in Him.

Happy is the one whose transgression is forgiven,
　　whose sin is pardoned.
Happy is the person unto whom God does not count
　　iniquity
And in whose spirit there is no guile.
While I kept silence, my bones degenerated
Through my groaning all day long.
For day and night Your hand was heavy upon me.
My sap was turned as in the droughts of summer,
　　Selah.
I confessed my sin to You,
And my iniquity have I not hid.
I said: "I will make confession concerning my
　　transgressions unto God,"
And You forgave the iniquity of my sin. Selah.
For this let everyone that is godly pray to You
In a time when You may be found.
Surely, when the great waters overflow, they will
　　not reach unto him.
You are my hiding place and will preserve me from
　　the enemy.
With songs of deliverance You will encircle me.
　　Selah.
I will instruct and teach you in the way that you
　　should go,
I will give counsel, My eye being upon you.
Do not be like the horse or mule that has no
　　understanding;
Whose mouth must be held in with bit and bridle,
That they come not near to you.
Many are the sorrows of the wicked;
But the one that trusts in God will have mercy
　　encircle him.
Rejoice in God, and be happy, you righteous ones;
Shout for joy, those that are upright in heart.

3. Psalm 41: This psalm, a type of sufferer's prayer, relates to a time of sickness when the patient's suffering was aggravated by mental uneasiness over the machinations of enemies. In particular, one person whom he had considered a close friend had proved traitorous. If the psalm truly mirrors an incident in David's life, the faithless friend may well have been Achitophel, and the time of its composition the uprising of David's son Absalom.

The psalm expresses David's thanks to God for having healed him. Only one who himself has suffered illness can appreciate what others who are sick are enduring. This should spur everyone to be understanding of the needs of the sick and to care for them appropriately.

> For the Leader. A Psalm of David.
> Happy is the one that considers the poor,
> God will deliver him in the day of evil.
> God preserves him, and keeps him alive
> Let him be called happy in the land.
> And do not deliver him into the greed of his
>   enemies.
> God supports him on the bed of sickness.
> May You turn all his lying down in sickness.
> As for me, I said: "O God, be gracious to me;
> Heal my soul, for I have sinned against You."
> My enemies speak evil things of me:
> "When shall he die, and his name perish?"
> And if one comes to see me, he speaks falsehood,
> His heart gathers iniquity to itself;
> When he goes abroad, he speaks of it.
> All that hate me whisper together against me,

Against me do they devise my hurt.
An evil thing cleaves strongly to him,
And now that he lies, he shall no more rise up.
My own familiar friend, in whom I trusted, who did
    eat of my bread,
Has lifted up his heel against me.
But You, O God, be gracious to me, and raise me up,
That I may requite them.
By this I know that You delight in me.
That my enemy does not triumph over me.
As for me, You uphold me because of my integrity
And set me before Your face forever.
Blessed is the Lord, the God of Israel,
From everlasting to everlasting. Amen and amen.

4. Psalm 42: This psalm features water as one of its main metaphors. Water has the power to nourish, but also has the power to be a terribly destructive force. The soul of the psalmist is tormented, and he yearns for communion with God. He acknowledges that he is in the depths of depression, but in the end comes to the realization that God will direct the flood of troubles and will see that he is not drowned in them.

For the Leader, Maskil of the sons of Korach.
As the hart pants after the water brooks
So pants my soul after You, O God.
My soul thirsts for God, for the living God,
"When shall I come and appear before God?"
My tears have been my food day and night
While they say unto me, all the day: "Where is your
    God?"
These things I remember, and pour out my soul
    within me,

How I passed on with the throng, and led them to
    the house of God,
With the voice of joy and praise, a multitude
    keeping holy day.
Why are you cast down, O my soul?
And why moan you within me?
Hope in God, for I shall yet praise Him
For the salvation of God's countenance.
O my God, my soul is cast down within me;
Therefore do I remember You from the land of
    Jordan,
And the Hermon, from the hill Mizar.
Deep calls unto deep at the voice of Your cataracts.
All Your waves and Your billows are gone over me.
By day God will command His lovingkindness,
And in the night God's song shall be with me,
Even a prayer to the God of my life.
I will say to God my Rock:
"Why have you forgotten me?
Why do I go mourning under the oppression
    of the enemy?"
As with a crushing in my bones, my enemies taunt me;
While they say to me all the day: "Where is your God?"
Why are you cast down, O my soul?
And why do you moan within me?
Hope in God, for I shall yet praise Him,
The salvation of my countenance, and my God.

5. Psalm 59: This psalm, in the form of a prayer in
time of danger, is said to have been written about
the time that David fled from the wrath of King
Saul. God's help is invoked as David prays that the
enemy will be destroyed, thus manifesting God's
righteousness in judgment. His faith and trust in

God fill him with song at the conclusion of the psalm.

For the Leader; *Al tashcheth*. A Psalm of David.
When Saul sent and they watched the house to kill
  him.
Deliver me from my enemies, O my God;
Set me on high from them that rise up against me.
Deliver me from the workers of iniquity,
Save me from the men of blood.
For lo, they lie in wait for my soul,
The impudent gather themselves together against me.
Not for my transgressions, nor for my sin, O God.
Without my fault, they run and prepare themselves,
Awake to help me, and behold.
You, therefore, O God of hosts, the God of Israel,
Arouse Yourself to punish all the nations.
Show no mercy to any iniquitous traitors. Selah.
They return at evening, they howl like a dog,
And go around the city.
Beyond, they belch out with their mouth,
Swords are in their lips:
"For who does hear?"
But You, O God, shall laugh at them
You shall have all the nations in derision.
Because of his strength, I will wait for You,
For God is my high tower.
The God of mercy will come to meet me,
God will let me gaze upon my enemies.
Do not slay them, lest my people forget,
Make them wander to and fro by Your power,
Bring them down, O God our shield.
For the sin of their mouth, and the words of their
  lips,
Let them even be taken in their pride,

And for cursing and lying which they speak.
Consume them in wrath, consume them, that they
   be no more.
And let them know that God rules in Jacob,
Unto the ends of the earth. Selah.

6. Psalm 77: In this psalm of deep anguish, the writer gives voice to the people in a time of national eclipse. According to the commentator Rashi, the occasion is, most likely, the Babylonian captivity. The cause of the writer's mental and spiritual distress is that he dares to imagine that God is capable of casting off His people. At the psalm's conclusion, the writer recalls all the wonders that God had previously performed for the Israelites, including the miracle of the parting of the Red Sea. This provides the writer with an emotional lift as he reminds himself that God can and will continue to perform wonders for the people of Israel.

For the Leader, for Yedutaun. A Psalm of Asaf.
I will lift my voice to God and cry,
I will lift up my voice to God,
So that God may hear me.
In the day of my trouble I seek God,
With my hand uplifted, my eye cries at night with
   stopping.
My soul refuses to be comforted.
When I think thereon, O God, I must moan,
When I muse thereon, my spirit faints. Selah.
You hold fast the lids of my eyes;
I am troubled, unable to speak.
I have pondered the days of old,
The years of ancient times.

In the night I will call to remembrance my song;
I will commune with my own heart,
And my spirit makes diligent search.
Will God cast off forever?
Will God be favorable no more?
Is God's mercy gone forever?
Is God's promise come to an end forevermore?
Has God forgotten to be gracious?
Has God in anger shut up His compassion? Selah.
And I say: "This is my weakness,
That the right hand of the Most High could change.
I will make mention of the deeds of God,
I will remember Your wonders of old.
I will also meditate upon all Your work,
And muse on Your doings."
O God, Your way is in holiness;
Who is a great god like You, O God?
You are the God that does wonders,
You have made known Your strength among the
      peoples.
You have with Your arm redeemed Your people,
The sons of Jacob and Joseph. Selah.
The waters saw You, O God,
The waters saw You, they were in pain,
The depths also trembled.
The clouds flooded forth waters,
The skies sent out a sound,
Your arrows also went abroad.
The voice of Your thunder was in the whirlwind,
The lightnings lighted up the world,
The earth trembled and quaked.
Your way was in the sea,
And Your path in the great waters,
And your footsteps were not known.
You did lead Your people like a flock,
By the hand of Moses and Aaron.

7. Psalm 90: This psalm dwells upon the transitory character of a person's existence, but not pessimistically. If life is brief, its moments are precious and must not be wasted in ineffectual pursuits. The cause of human disease is God's anger, and the writer asks God to help him understand the consequences that follow the spending of life's opportunities in unworthy ways. The psalm concludes with a prayer for the return of God's favor and a desire for God to invest human striving with some of God's own enduring power.

A Prayer of Moses, the man of God.
God, You have been our dwelling place in all
   generations.
Before the mountains were brought forth,
Or ever You had formed the Earth and the world,
Even from everlasting to everlasting, You are God.
You turn man to contrition
And say: "Return, you children of men."
For a thousand years in Your sight
Are but as yesterday when it is past,
And as a watch in the night.
You carry them away as with a flood, they are as
   a sleep,
In the morning they are like grass which grows up.
In the morning it flourishes and grows up,
In the evening it is cut down and withers.
For we are consumed in Your anger,
and by Your wrath are we hurried away.
You have set our iniquities before You,
Our secret sins in the light of Your countenance.
For all our days are passed away in Your anger,
We bring our years to an end as a tale that is told.

The days of our years are three score years and ten,
Or even by reason of strength four score years,
Yet is their pride but travail and vanity,
For it is speedily gone, and we fly away.
Who knows the power of Your anger,
And Your wrath according to the fear that is due
     to You?
So teach us to number our days,
That we may get us a heart of wisdom.
Return, O God, how long?
And let it repent You concerning Your servants.
O satisfy us in the morning with Your mercy,
That we may rejoice and be glad all our days.
Make us glad according to the days wherein You
     have afflicted us,
According to the years wherein we have seen evil.
Let Your work appear unto Your servants,
And Your glory upon their children.
And let the graciousness of the Lord our God be
     upon us,
May the work of our hands be established,
Establish the work of our hands.

8. Psalm 105: This psalm gives a retrospect of God's dealings with Abraham and his descendants to the time of their taking possession of the Promised Land. It is believed to have been composed after the return from captivity, when the minds of the Israelites were appropriately directed to the early history of the nation and God's part in it. The first part of the psalm is the writer's exhortation to praise God, while the second part of the psalm deals with the theme of God's protection of the Patriarchs. The psalm concludes with the citation of several of the plagues that befell the Egyptians in Egypt and God's care of the Israelites in the wilderness. In commenting on this psalm, Rabbi Maurice Lamm concludes that the psalm teaches people ways to heal, including the suggestions that people must not allow themselves to sink into victimhood and that, by singing songs to God, one can raise one's soul, which aids in the healing process.

Give thanks to God, call upon God's name,
Make known God's doings among the peoples.
Sing to God, sing praises to Him,
Speak of all of God's wondrous works.
Glory in God's holy name,
Let the heart of them rejoice that seeks God.
Seek God and His strength,
Seek God's face continually.
Remember God's marvelous works that He has
   done,
God's wonders, and the judgments of God's mouth.
O you seed of Abraham His servant,
You children of Jacob, God's chosen ones.
He is the Lord our God,
His judgments are in all the earth.
He has remembered His covenant forever,
The word which He commanded to a thousand
   generations.
The covenant which God made with Abraham,
And God's oath to Isaac,
And God established it for Jacob as a statute,
To Israel for an everlasting covenant.
Saying: "Unto you will I give the land of Canaan,"
The lot of your inheritance.

When they were but a few men in number,
Yea, very few, and sojourners in it,
And when they went about from nation to nation,
From one kingdom to another people,
God suffered no person to do them wrong,
Yea, for their sake God reproved kings.
"Touch not My anointed ones,
And do not harm My prophets."
And God called a family upon the land,
God broke the whole staff of bread.
God sent a man before them,
Joseph was sold for a servant.
His feet they hurt with fetters,
His person was laid in iron.
Until the time that his word came to pass,
The word of God tested him.
The king sent and loosed him,
Even the ruler of peoples, and set him free.
He made him lord of his house,
And ruler of all his possessions.
To bind his princes at his pleasure,
And teach his elders wisdom.
Israel also came into Egypt,
And Jacob sojourned in the land of Ham.
And God increased His people enormously,
And made them too mighty for their enemies.
God turned their heart to hate His people,
To deal craftily with His servants.
God sent Moses His servant,
And Aaron whom God had chosen.
They wrought among them His manifold signs,
And wonders in the land of Ham.
God sent darkness, and it was dark,
And they rebelled not against God's word.
God turned their waters into blood,

And slew their fish.
Their land swarmed with frogs,
In the chambers of their kings.
God spoke, and there came forth swarms of flies,
And gnats in all of their borders.
God gave them hail for rain,
And flaming fire in their land.
God smote their vines also and their fig trees,
And broke the trees of their borders,
God spoke, and the locust came,
And the canker worm without numbers.
He did eat up every herb in their land,
And did eat up the fruit of their ground.
God smote also all the firstborn in their land,
The first fruits of all their strength.
And God brought them forth with silver and gold,
And there was none that stumbled among God's
    tribes.
Egypt was glad when they departed,
For the fear of them had fallen upon them.
God spread a cloud for a screen,
And fire to give light in the night.
They asked, and God brought quails,
And gave them in abundance the bread of heaven.
God opened the rock and waters spewed forth,
They ran, a river in the dry places.
For God remembered His holy word,
Unto Abraham His servant.
And God brought forth His people with joy,
His chosen ones with singing.
And God gave them the lands of the nations,
And they took the labor of the peoples in
    possession,
That they might keep God's statutes and observe
    God's laws. Hallelujah.

9. Psalm 137: The feelings that moved the psalmist will be best understood if we think of him as an exile recently returned from Babylon, visiting with horror the devastation wreaked upon the city he so dearly loved. Lines 5 and 6 of the psalm point to the importance of continuing to sing, and the thought of Jerusalem brings the exiled people happiness, The promise of hope, and a modicum of spiritual healing.

By the rivers of Babylon,
There we sat down and cried,
When we remembered Zion.
Upon the willows in the midst thereof
We hung up our harps.
For there they that led us captive asked us words
    of song,
And our tormentors asked of us mirth:
"Sing us one of the songs of Zion."
How shall we sing God's song,
In a foreign land?
If I forget you, O Jerusalem,
Let my right hand forget her cunning.
Let my tongue cleave to the roof of my mouth,
If I do not remember you.
If I have not set Jerusalem above my chiefest joy.
Remember, O God, against the children of Edom,
The day of Jerusalem,
Who said: "Raze it, raze it,
Even to the foundation thereof."
O daughter of Babylon, that is to be destroyed.
Happy shall he be, that repays you
As you have served us.
Happy shall he be, that takes and dashes your little
    ones against the rock.

10. Psalm 150: The final psalm is Psalm 150, often called the musical psalm. It mentions many of the instruments that were played during Temple times and were used to praise God. Rabbi Nachman of Breslov challenges those who are ill to continue to sing to God, even in time of illness. With its concluding call "to everything that has breath," the psalmist sums up the aspiration and aim of Israel's mission and the purpose of its existence as God's appointed messenger to humanity.

Hallelujah. Praise God in His sanctuary,
Praise Him in the firmament of His power.
Praise God for His mighty acts,
Praise God for His abundant greatness.
Praise God with the blast of the horn,
Praise God with the psaltery and harp.
Praise God with the timbrel and dance,
Praise God with stringed instruments and the lute.
Praise God with the loud sounding cymbals,
Praise God with the clanging cymbals.
Let everything that has breath praise God
Hallelujah.

A SELECTION OF PSALMS IN TIME OF ILLNESS

There are other psalms, aside from the ten previously enumerated, that can be said by those who are ill and those who are bedridden with illness. Following are some of the better-known ones.

1. Psalm 6: Commentators state that this psalm was composed when David was bedridden with a terrible illness. But David did not dedicate it to himself alone; rather, he meant it as a prayer for every person in distress, particularly those who are sick or oppressed in exile.

> For the Leader, with string music on the *Sheminit*.
> A Psalm of David.
> O God, do not rebuke me in Your anger,
> Neither chasten me in Your wrath.
> Be gracious to me, O God, for I languish away,
> Heal me, O God, for my bones are terrified.
> My soul is sore affrighted,
> And You, O God, how long?
> Return, O God, deliver my soul,
> Save me for Your mercy's sake.
> For in death there is no remembrance of You,
> In the nether world who will give You thanks.
> I am weary with groaning.
> Every night I cause my bed to swim;
> I melt away my couch with my tears.
> My eye is dimmed because of vexation;
> It waxes old because of all of my enemies.
> Depart from me, all you workers of transgression.
> For God has heard the voice of weeping.
> God has heard my supplication,
> God receives my prayer.
> All my enemies shall be ashamed and afraid,
> They shall turn back, they shall be suddenly
>   ashamed.

2. Psalm 38: In this psalm, David recognizes that his illness is a result of his transgressions. This recognition alone can spur a person to repentance, which can then be the cause for God's grace and deliverance. At the same time, a person can benefit from his illness by being made to realize that good health is not to be taken for granted; that it is, rather, a divine blessing dependent upon one's good deeds.

A Psalm of David, to make a memorial.
O God, do not rebuke me in Your anger,
Neither chasten me in Your wrath.
For Your arrows are gone deep into me,
And Your hand is come down upon me.
There is no soundness in my flesh because of Your
     indignation,
Neither is there any health in my bones because of
     my sin.
For my iniquities are gone over my head,
As a heavy burden they are too heavy for me.
My wounds are noisome, they fester,
Because of my foolishness.
I am bent and bowed down greatly,
I go mourning all the day.
For my loins are filled with burning,
And there is no soundness in my flesh.
I am benumbed and sore crushed,
I groan by reason of the moaning of my heart.
God, all my desire is before You,
And my sighing is not hid from You.
My heart flutters, my strength fails me,
As for the light of my eyes, it also is gone from me.
My friends and my companions stand aloof from my
     plague,
And my kinsmen stand afar off.

They also that seek after my life lay snares for me,
And they that seek my hurt speak crafty devices,
And utter deceits all the day.
But I am as a deaf person, I do not hear,
And I am as a dumb man that opens not his mouth.
Yea, I am become as a man that hears not,
And in whose mouth are no arguments.
For in You, O God, do I hope,
You will answer, O Lord my God.
For I said: "Lest they rejoice over me;
When my foot slips, they magnify themselves
    against me."
For I am ready to halt,
And my pain is continually before me.
For I do declare my iniquity,
I am full of care because of my sin.
But my enemies are strong in health,
And they that hate me wrongfully are multiplied.
They also that repay evil for good
Are adversaries unto me, because I follow the thing
    that is good.
Forsake me not, O God,
O my God, do not be far away from me.
Make haste to help me,
O God of my salvation.

3. Psalm 88: This psalm describes the agonies of
exile and Israel's impassioned plea for divine deliverance. It is appropriate to use in beseeching
God to deliver one from any sort of illness or
distress.

A song, a Psalm of the sons of Korach,
For the Leader, upon Machalat Leanot.

Maskil of Heman the Ezrachite.
O Lord, God of my salvation;
What time I cry in the night before You.
Let my prayer come before You,
Incline Your ear unto my cry.
For my soul is sated with troubles,
and my life draws near to the grave.
I am counted with them that go down to the pit,
I am become as a man that has no help.
Set apart among the dead,
Like the slain that lie in the grave,
Whom You remember no more,
And they are cut off from Your hand.
You have laid me in the nethermost pit,
In dark places, in the deeps.
Your wrath lies hard upon me,
And all Your waves You press down. Selah.
You have put my acquaintance far from me,
You have made me an abomination to them,
I am shut up, and I cannot come forth.
My eye languishes by reason of affliction,
I have called upon You, O God every day.
I have spread forth my hands to You.
Will You work wonders for the dead?
Or shall the shades arise and give You thanks?
    Selah.
Shall Your mercy be declared in the grave,
Or Your faithfulness in destruction?
Shall Your wonders be known in the dark?
And Your righteousness in the land of
    forgetfulness?
But as for me, unto You, O God do I cry,
And in the morning does my prayer come to meet
    You.
God, why do You cast off my soul?

Why do You hide Your face from me?
I am afflicted and at the point of death from my
    youth up,
I have borne Your terrors, I am distracted.
Your fierce anger is gone over me,
Your terrors have cut me off.
They came round about me like water all the day.
They compassed me about together.
Friend and companion have You put far from me,
And my acquaintance into darkness.

4. Psalm 91: This psalm speaks of the protection and help that one who believes in God will find. It offers hope to one who is in danger or struck by illness, and comfort to the bereaved, for it also alludes to the eternal life in the world-to-come. The commentator Rashi asserts that Moses is the composer of this psalm.

O you who dwell in the shelter of the Most High,
And abide in the shadow of the Almighty.
I will say of God who is my refuge and fortress,
My God, in whom I trust.
That God will deliver you from the snare of the
    fowler
And from the ruinous pestilence.
God will cover you with His pinions,
And under His wings shall you take refuge.
God's truth is a shield and armor.
You shall not be afraid of the terror by night,
Nor of the arrow that flies by day.
Of the pestilence that walks in darkness,
Nor of the destruction that wastes at noon.
A thousand may fall at your side,

And ten thousand at your right hand,
It shall not come near to you.
Only with your eyes shall you behold,
And see the recompense of the wicked.
For you have made God who is my refuge,
Even the Most High, your habitation.
There shall no evil befall you,
Neither shall any plague come near your tent.
For God will give His angels charge over you,
To keep you in all your ways.
They shall bear you upon their hands,
Lest you dash your foot against a stone.
You shall tread upon the lion and asp,
The young lion and the serpent shall you trample
    under feet.
"Because he has set his love upon Me, therefore
    will I deliver him,
I will set him on high, because he has known My
    name.
God shall come upon Me, and I will answer him,
I will be with him in trouble.
I will rescue him, and bring him to honor.
With long life will I satisfy him,
And make him to behold My salvation."

5. Psalm 103: When a person is afflicted with illness or other distresses, he becomes aware that he is composed of both body and soul. Rising above the flesh, the soul recognizes God's infinite kindness and is calmed by the knowledge that God in His love for people can and will bring healing.

A Psalm of David.
Bless the Lord, O my soul,

And all that is within me, bless God's holy name.
Bless God, O my soul,
and forget not all God's benefits.
Who forgives all your iniquity,
Who heals all your diseases.
Who redeems your life from the pit,
Who encompasses you with kindness and tender
    mercies.
Who satisfies your old age with good things,
So that your youth is renewed like the eagle.
God executes righteousness,
And acts of justice for all that are oppressed.
God made known His ways to Moses,
His doings unto the children of Israel.
God is full of compassion and gracious,
Slow to anger and abundant in mercy.
God will not always contend,
Neither will God keep His anger forever.
God has not dealt with us after our sins,
Nor requited us according to our transgressions.
For as the heaven is high above the Earth,
So great is God's mercy toward them that fear Him.
As far as the east is from the west,
So far has God removed our transgressions from us.
As a father has compassion upon his children,
So has God compassion upon those who fear Him.
For God knows our frame,
God remembers that we are dust.
As for man, his days are as grass,
As a flower of the field, so he flourishes.
For the wind passes over it, and it is gone,
And the place thereof knows it no more.
But the mercy of God is from everlasting to
    everlasting upon them that fear Him,
And God's righteousness unto children's children.

To such as keep God's covenant,
And to those that remember God's precepts to do
  them.
God has established His throne in the heavens,
And His kingdom rules over all.
Bless God, you angels,
You mighty in strength, that fulfills His word,
Hearkening to the voice of God's word.
Bless God, all you hosts,
You that minister to Him and that do His pleasure,
Bless God, all you His works,
In all places of His dominion,
Bless God, O my soul.

6. Psalm 30: Modern commentators have agreed that this psalm is a testimony to God's mercy in time of sore distress. Later it was given a national interpretation and selected for use at the dedication of the Second Temple and subsequently at its rededication by the Maccabees.

A Psalm, a Song at the dedication of the House of
  David.
I will extol You, O Lord, for You have raised me up,
And have not suffered my enemies to rejoice over
  me.
O Lord my God, I cried to You and You healed me,
O God, you brought up my soul from the
  netherworld.
You did keep me alive, that I should not go down to
  the pit.
Sing praise to the Lord, O you His godly ones,
And give thanks to God's holy name.
For God's anger is but for a moment,

God's favor is for a lifetime.
Weeping may tarry at night
But joy comes at the dawn.
Now I have said in my security,
"I shall never be moved."
You have established, O God, in Your favor
My mountain as a stronghold,
You did hide Your face and I was afraid.
Unto You, O God did I call,
And unto God I made supplication.
What profit is there in my blood,
When I go down to the pit?
Shall the dust praise You? Shall it declare Your
    truth?
Hear, O God, and be gracious to me,
God, be my helper.
You did turn for me my mourning into dancing,
You did loose my sackcloth, and gird me with
    gladness.
So that my glory may sing praise to You, and not be
    silent,
O Lord my God, I will give thanks to you forever and
    ever.

7. Psalm 139: This psalm recounts God's greatness in the universe, recalling both God's omniscience and His omnipresence. The psalm's conclusion reminds the reader that God will not tolerate those who conduct their lives contrary to His will.

For the Leader, A Psalm of David.
O God, You have searched me, and known me.
You know my downsitting and my uprising,
You understand my thought from afar off.

You measure my going about and my lying down,
And are acquainted with all of my ways.
For there is not a word in my tongue,
But lo, O God, You know it altogether.
You have hemmed me in behind and before,
And laid Your hand on me.
Such knowledge is too wonderful for me,
Too high, I cannot attain it.
Whither shall I go from Your spirit?
Or whither shall I flee from Your presence?
If I ascend up into heaven, You are there,
If I make my bed in the netherworld, You are there.
If I take the wings of the morning,
And dwell in the uttermost parts of the sea.
Even there would Your hand lead me,
And Your right hand would hold me.
And I say: "Surely the darkness shall envelop me,
And the light about me shall be night";
Even the darkness is not too dark for You,
But the night shines as the day,
The darkness is even as the light.
For You have made my mind,
You have knit me together in my mother's womb.
I will give thanks unto You, for I am fearfully and
    wonderfully made;
Wonderful are Your works,
And that my soul knows well.
My frame was not hidden from You,
When I was made in secret,
And curiously wrought in the lowest parts of the
    earth.
Your eyes did see my unformed substance,
And in Your book they were all written.
Even the days that were fashioned,
When as yet there was none of them.

How weighty also are Your thoughts unto me,
  O God.
How great is the sum of them.
If I would count them, they are more in number
  than the sand,
Were I to come to the end of them, I would still be
  with You.
If You but would slay the wicked, O God,
Depart from me, therefore, you men of blood,
Who utter Your name with wicked thought,
They take it for falsehood, even Your enemies.
Do not I hate them, O God, that hate You?
And do not I strive with those that rise up against
  You?
I hate them with utmost hatred,
I count them my enemies.
Search me, O God, and know my heart,
Try me, and know my thoughts.
And see if there be any way in me that is grievous,
And lead me in the way everlasting.

8. Psalm 27: This psalm traditionally has been appointed for recital daily throughout the month of Elul (the month preceding Rosh Hashanah) as preparation for the coming of the New Year and the Day of Atonement. It proclaims God the Protector, and offers healing to the sick by reminding the reader that God's protective care of His creatures is even more constant than that of parents for their child.

A Psalm of David.
The Lord is my light and my salvation, whom shall
  I fear?

The Lord is the stronghold of my life, of whom shall
   I be afraid?
When evil doers came upon me to eat my flesh,
Even my enemies and my foes, they stumbled and
   fell.
Though a host should encamp against me, my heart
   shall not fear,
Though war were waged against me, even then I
   would be confident.
One thing have I asked of the Lord, this do I desire,
That I may dwell in the house of the Lord all the
   days of my life.
To behold the graciousness of the Lord,
To visit early in His temple.
For He conceals me in His pavilion in the day of
   evil,
He hides me in the shelter of His tent,
He lifts me up upon a rock.
Now shall my head be lifted up above my enemies
   round about me.
And I will offer in His tabernacle sacrifices with
   trumpet sound,
I will sing, yea I will sing praises to God.
Hear, O God, when I call with my voice,
Be gracious to me, and answer me.
In Your behalf my heart has said:
"Seek My face";
Your face, O God, I will seek.
Hide not Your face from me,
Put not Your servant away in anger,
You have been my help
Cast me not off, nor forsake me, O God of my
   salvation.
For though my father and my mother have forsaken
   me,

God will take me up.
Teach me Your way, O God,
And lead me in an even path,
Because of them that lie in wait for me.
Deliver me not over unto the will of my enemies,
For false witnesses have risen against me, and such
    as breathe out violence,
If I had not believed to look upon the goodness of
    God
In the land of the living.
Wait for the Lord,
Be strong and let your heart take courage,
Yea, wait for the Lord.

NOTABLE QUOTATIONS
ON HEALING

O God, heal her now, I beseech You (Numbers 12:13).

Following is a set of quotations that shed light on a facet of healing as portrayed in the Bible, rabbinic teaching, and the liturgy.

IMAGES OF GOD AS HEALER

These are quotations whose themes relate images of God as Healer, images of God as being compassionate and close to people, and liturgical responses to God as Healer.

1. And God appeared to Abram by the terebinths of Mamre, as he sat in the tent in the heat of the day (Genesis 18:10). [The rabbis connect this sentence with the preceding verses in Genesis 17, and declare that God visited the Patriarch during the indisposition that resulted from his circumcision. From this passage they deduce the religious duty of visiting the sick, which can help to heal a person.]

2. I will put none of the diseases upon you that I have put upon the Egyptians, for I am the Lord that heals you (Exodus 15:26).

3. God has torn and God will heal us (Hosea 6:1).

4. In the world-to-come, the Holy Blessed One will cure the world, as it states: "I will restore health to you, and I will heal you of your wounds" [Isaiah 30:26]. God will cure all the ills of the world (Ecclesiastes Rabbah 7:1).

5. Rabbi Alexandri said: "If a person uses broken vessels, it is considered an embarrassment. But God seeks out broken vessels for His use, as it says: 'God is the healer of shattered hearts' [Psalms 147:3]" (Leviticus Rabbah 7:2).

6. I will be with him in time of trouble (Psalms 91:15). [That is, when Israel feels pain, God will always be there.]

7. God hears the cry of all humanity (*Mechilta Masechta de-Shirah* 4).

8. Heal us, O God, and we shall be healed (*Amidah*).

9. And Moses cried to God saying: "Heal her now, O God, I beseech you" (Numbers 12:13).

GOD AS PARTNER
IN ISRAEL'S TRAVAIL

The following quotations relate to God's empathy for His people. These quotations suggest that God cannot heal alone, but needs humanity's participation as well.

1. Whenever the Holy One calls to mind His children deep in travail among the nations of the world, He—if one dare say this—lets fall two tears into the Great Sea. Their splash is heard from world's end to world's end, and that is the cause of earthquakes (Berachot 59a).

2. "My dove, My twin" [Song of Songs 5:2]. Rabbi Yannai said: "As with twins, when the head of one aches, the other also feels it, so too, if one dare utter such a thing, the Holy One said, 'I am with him in trouble' [Psalms 91:15]. And again, 'In all their affliction, He too was afflicted' [Isaiah 63:9]. The Holy One said to Moses: 'Are you not aware that I am wracked with pain even as Israel is wracked with pain? Take note of the place whence I speak to you—from the midst of a thornbush. I am'—if one may ascribe such a statement of God—'a partner in their pain'" (Exodus Rabbah 2:5).

3. Pause and consider how plentiful always are the mercies of the Holy One for the people of Israel. For in any generation that you find righ-

teous, faithful, and worthy men grieving in exile, the Holy One claps both hands together, then He clasps them over His heart, and then He folds His arms as He weeps secretly for the righteous. Why does He weep for them secretly? Because it is unseemly for a lion to weep before a fox, unseemly for a sage to weep before his disciple, unseemly for a king to weep before the least of his servants, as is said, "So that you will not hear it, My soul shall weep in secret" [Jeremiah 13:17] (*Seder Eliyah Rabbah*).

4. "Open to Me, My sister, My love, My dove, My undefiled; for My head is filled with dew" [Song of Songs 5:2]. In the time to come, when the Holy One comes to redeem Israel, they will say: "Master of the Universe, You exiled us among the nations and thrust us out of Your house. And now You come to redeem us?" The Holy One will reply: "I will tell you the parable of a king who divorced his wife and the next day came to bring her back. She said: 'My lord king, yesterday you drove me out of your house, and today you come to take me back?' He said: 'You should know that since you left my house, I, too, have not gone into my house. If you do not believe me, look at the dew on my head.'" Likewise, the Holy One will say to Israel: "Ever since the day you left My house, I, too, have not gone into My house. If you do not believe Me, put your hands upon My head, and you will see that 'My head is filled with dew, My locks with the drops of the night'" (Midrash based on *Yalkut Eliezer* 68).

TORAH AS THERAPY
FOR HEALING

In these quotations, we see how God works as a Healer through His gift of Torah.

1. There is no affliction for which a cure does not exist. The therapy and medicine for every ill is discernible. If you see that misfortune not befall your body, study Torah, for it is therapy for the whole body (Midrash Tanchuma Vitro 8).

2. Our masters taught: "Therefore shall you lay up (vesamtem) these My words" [Deuteronomy 11:18]. The word samtem is to be understood as a compound of sam (remedy), and tam (perfect), the Torah being compared to a lifesaving remedy. A parable of a man who gave his son a severe blow and then put a plaster on the sore spot, saying: "My son, so long as this plaster is on your sore, you may eat what you like, drink what you like, bathe in hot or cold water, and need not be afraid. But if you remove it, the sore will open up." So, too, the Holy One said to Israel: "My children, I created the impulse to evil and I created the Torah as its antidote. If you occupy yourselves with Torah, you will not be delivered into the power of the impulse to evil, for the Bible says, 'If you occupy yourself with that which is good, you will be exalted'" [Genesis 4:7] (Kiddushin 30b).

3. Rabbi Judah son of Rabbi Chiyya said: "Pause and consider how the effect of human action is not

at all like the effect of the Holy One's action. In human action, when a man gives a drug to his fellow, it may be beneficial to one part of the body but injurious to another. Not so the Holy One: He gave Israel the Torah, a lifesaving drug for the entire body, as is said, 'healing to all his flesh'" [Proverbs 4:22] (*Eruvin* 54a).

4. Rabbi Joshua ben Levi said: "When a man is on a journey and has no company, let him occupy himself with study of Torah, for the Bible says, 'They are to be companions of grace' [Proverbs 1:9] When a man feels pain in his head, let him occupy himself with Torah. . . . When he feels pain in his entire body, let him occupy himself with Torah, since another verse speaks of it as 'healing for his whole body'" [Proverbs 4:22] (*Eurvin* 54a).

5. "These are the words" [*devarim*] (Deuteronomy 1:1). Just as bees [*devorim*] reserve their honey for their owner and their sting for others, so are words of Torah an elixir of life for Israel, but deadly poison for the nations of the earth (Deuteronomy Rabbah 1:6).

6. Rabbi Judah said in the name of Samuel: "What is meant by 'You make men as the flesh of the sea' [Habbakuk 1:14]? In what way can men be spoken of as being like fish of the sea? In this way: As the fish of the sea, once they go up on dry land, promptly die, so human beings, as soon as they give up Torah and its precepts, promptly die" (*Avodah Zarah* 3a).

7. We have been taught: "They went three days in the wilderness, and found no water" [Exodus 15:22]. Those who expound the inner meaning of the Bible say that here "water" can mean only Torah, of which it is written, "Everyone that thirsts, come for water" [Isaiah 55:1] (*Baba Kamma* 82a).

PRAYERS FOR HEALING

1. May it be Your will, O Lord my God, that this operation be a cure for me. May You heal me, for You are a faithful healing God; Your healing is sure, since people have no power to heal but this is a habit to them.

2. O God, we beseech You, heal her now (Numbers 12:13).

3. Heal us, O Lord, and we shall be healed. Help us and save us, for You are our glory. Grant perfect healing for all our afflictions (*Amidah*).

4. May He who blessed our ancestors, Abraham, Isaac, and Jacob, Sarah, Rebecca, Rachel, and Leah, bless and heal———. May the Holy One in mercy strengthen him (her) and heal him (her) soon, body and soul, together with others who suffer illness. And let us say: Amen (traditional *Mi Shebayrach* prayer of healing for the ill).

5. In sickness I turn to You, O God, for comfort and help. Strengthen within me the wondrous power

of healing that You have implanted in Your children. Guide my doctors and nurses that they may speed my recovery. Let my dear ones find comfort and courage in the knowledge that You are with us at all times, in sickness as in health. May my sickness not weaken my faith in You, nor diminish my love for others. From my illness may I gain a fuller sympathy for all who suffer. I praise You, O God, the Source of healing (excerpted from *On the Doorposts of Your House*, Chaim Stern, ed.).

For Further Reading

Abraham, A. S. *Medical Halacha for Everyone.* Jerusalem: Feldheim Publishers, 1980.

Blanchard, Tsvi. *Joining Heaven and Earth. Maimonides and the Laws of Bikkur Cholim.* New York: National Center for Jewish Healing, 1996.

Bleich, J. David. *Judaism and Healing.* New York: Ktav Publishers, 1981.

Borowitz, Eugene B. *Please, God, Heal Her, Please.* New York: Hebrew Union College—Jewish Institute of Religion, Jewish Theological Seminary, Reconstructionist Rabbinical College and National Center for Jewish Healing, 1997.

Friedenwald, H. *The Jews and Medicine* (vol. 1). Baltimore: Johns Hopkins Press, 1944.

Ganzfried, Solomon. *Code of Jewish Law (Condensed Version).* New York: Hebrew Publishing Company, 1961.

HeChasid, Rabbi Yehudah. *Sefer Chasidim: The Book of the Pious.* (trans. by Avraham Yaakov Finkel). Northvale, New Jersey: Jason Aronson, 1997.

Jakobovits, Immanuel. *Jewish Medical Ethics.* New York: Bloch Publishers, 1975.

Katz, Nina Dubler. *A Training Manual for Bikur Cholim Volunteers*. New York: Council on Bikur Cholim of Greater New York, n.d.

Kensky, Tikva Frymer. *Constructing a Theology of Healing*. New York: Hebrew Union College— Jewish Institute of Religion, Jewish Theological Seminary, Reconstructionist Rabbinical College and National Center for Jewish Healing, 1997.

Levine, Aaron. *How to Perform the Great Mitzvah of Bikur Cholim*. Toronto: Zikhron Meir, 1987.

Maimonides. *The Preservation of Youth*. New York: Philosophical Library, 1958.

———. *Mishneh Torah, The Book of Knowledge. Hilchot De'ot*. Jerusalem: Boys Town Jerusalem Publishers, 1962.

Novick, Bernard. *Making Jewish Decisions About the Body*. New York: United Synagogue of Conservative Judaism Department of Youth Activities, 1994.

Ozarowski, Joseph S. *To Walk in God's Ways—Jewish Pastoral Perspectives on Illness and Bereavement*. Northvale, New Jersey: Jason Aronson, 1995.

Prayers for Healing. Bridgeport, Connecticut: Prayer Book Press of Medica Judaica, Inc., n.d.

Rosner, Fred. *Medicine in the Bible and the Talmud*. New York: Ktav Publishers and Yeshiva University Press, 1977.

Selikovitsch, G. *Memorial Prayers and Meditations*. New York: Hebrew Publishing Company, 1910.

Stern, Chaim (ed.). *On the Doorposts of Your House*. New York: Central Conference of American Rabbis, 1994.

Weinstein, Joshua. *Maimonides the Educator*. New York: Pedagogic Library, 1970.

Weintraub, Simkha Y. (ed.). *Healing of Soul, Healing of Body*. Woodstock, Vermont: Jewish Lights Publishing, 1994.

Zabra, Joseph ben Meir. *Sefer Shaashu'im*. (Israel Davidson ed.). New York: Jewish Theological Seminary, 1914.

Index

About the Author

Rabbi Ronald Isaacs is the spiritual leader of Temple Sholom in Bridgewater, New Jersey. He received his doctorate in instructional technology from Columbia University's Teacher's College. He is the author of numerous books, including *Loving Companions: Our Jewish Wedding Album*, co-authored with Leora Isaacs. Rabbi Isaacs currently serves on the editorial board of *Shofar* magazine and is a member of the Publications Committee of the Rabbinical Assembly. He resides in New Jersey with his wife, Leora, and their children, Keren and Zachary.